THE
LANGUAGE
GAP
AND GOD

THE LANGUAGE GAP AND GOD

Religious Language and
Christian Education

Randolph Crump Miller

Pilgrim Press

Philadelphia   Boston

SBN 8298–0180–4
Library of Congress Catalog Card No. 72–126863

Copyright © 1970 United Church Press
Philadelphia, Pennsylvania

To Rives

Contents

ix

Preface

This book is written for Christian educators, trainers, teachers, and lay people who are facing the question: "How can we say what we mean about God so that our assertions will be understood, accepted, and responded to?" When we speak of God, many people do not realize what the word means or to whom it points. The influence of Western technological culture has infiltrated the thinking of educated people throughout the world and the categories of secular concepts are used to explain everything from repairing a bicycle to interpreting the scriptures.

Part of the problem lies in the nature of religious language. We have become aware of the difficulty of communicating the mythic images of the Bible, due partly to Rudolf Bultmann's theory of demythologizing, but the difficulty is more likely with the language itself. The high poetry of the Gospels is often considered to be fantasy by those who think only within the limited framework of verification of sense experience. Even when liturgical forms are deeply moving, the emotional response is not considered to be grounded in reality.

Within the Christian community, there are many who are at home with the traditional forms, which continue to have meaning for the initiated. These people tend to resent the efforts to communicate in new words and liturgical acts, object to translations of the Bible into current language, and fail to see the distinctions between various categories of language usage. Yet, they find increasing difficulty in communicating what they believe in societies influenced by modern secularism or by differing religious viewpoints.

One important resource, it seems to me, for overcoming

some of these difficulties, is language analysis, a philosophical study of the use and meaning of language. Words and sentences are used in different ways in order to express various levels of thinking. We work by means of systems of words, and these systems cannot be mixed except with the greatest care. These systems or categories of language usage are called language-games by Wittgenstein. Each language-game has its own logic and means of verification, and it is important to establish the logical placing of the language of faith.

This book is not a critical study of language analysis. It is an attempt to present the findings of such study in terms of their application to Christian education. In each chapter, a survey is made of a significant view of the use of language, followed by comments on the educational implications. We are concerned with the use and meaning of language for the purpose of Christian education. This book is an extension of the thinking that began in a portion of chapter 5 of my *Christian Nurture and the Church* (1961) and presupposes the overall theory of Christian nurture espoused there.

It is important to recognize the self-imposed limitations of this study. We are to deal with the key problem of how to talk about God, as this issue is illuminated by our understanding of how religious language works. This book does not pretend to offer a full-fledged doctrine of God; it deals with the doctrine of Christ only in passing; it mentions other doctrines by illustration. The full picture can be seen in other books I have written.

The approach is straightforward. We begin with a summary of the language of the Gospels, recognizing that Christianity is what might be called a speech-event. Then we turn to a survey of early language analysis, drawing on Paul van Buren's development of this kind of thinking and his views of Christian education. This sets the stage for asking if there is a God who exists about whom we may talk, and at this point we rely on the writings of F. S. C. Northrop, Alfred North Whitehead, and Charles Hartshorne, and then we consider the educational results of their approach. Against this background, we begin a consideration of the use of language with the study of biblical myth, relying on Bultmann and Schubert Ogden, and we see what religious discourse means for Christian education according to Bultmann or Ogden or Amos Wilder. Now we are ready for more constructive suggestions, beginning with Ian T. Ramsey's analysis of religious language as logically odd, a kind of speaking which may evoke a disclosure and lead to a commitment; his own examples provide an approach to how Christian education works through models and qualifiers. This approach is continued from another perspective in the thinking of Horace Bushnell and Francis H. Drinkwater who work through the language of the heart and provide us with the category of poetic-simple. But language does more than produce disclosures or reach the heart, and in the thinking of Donald Evans we come to the self-involving and rapportive language that does things; this gives us an opportunity to see how a changed onlook can lead to effective confirmation results. This problem of change in persons is looked at again in the next chapter, using the convenient labels of bliks and onlooks as a basis for seeing what education can do as initiation. One step beyond this is the issue of how one looks on God and his world, which brings in the problem of a world view in which Christian education can operate effectively today. The concluding chapter seeks to wrap up the discussion by consideration of the thinking of Reuel L. Howe, David R. Hunter, and Gerard S. Sloyan in Christian education, followed by a brief treatment of worship and ecumenical education.

This approach is, I hope, not too technical. I have omitted most of the difficult jargon, the critical evaluations, and the detailed extension of the arguments. The primary purpose is to use these insights in order that the verbal side of Christian teaching may be more effective. Certainly, if we take these findings seriously, we who teach will avoid many of the worst blunders. At least, we will be conscious of the language-game we are using and will assist our students in understanding how we point and show in religious language in a way that is different from how we do so in a chemistry laboratory.

The reading of Ian T. Ramsey's *Religious Language* (1957) started my thinking in the direction of the thesis of this book. In 1965, I gave a seminar covering some of this material at Union Theological College, Vancouver, B.C. The following fall, I repeated the seminar at Yale Divinity School, and for this I wrote a paper on "Linguistic Models and Christian Education," which I later read at the Professors and Research Section of the National Council of Churches and published in *Religious Education* for July–August 1966. The seminar was repeated at Union Theological Seminary in the summer of 1966, at Yale in the fall of 1967 and 1969, and at Drew in the fall of 1968.

A sabbatical year gave me the opportunity to do some additional study while teaching at Serampore College, India, and later at the Near East School of Theology, Beirut. Schubert Ogden, Donald Evans, and Paul van Buren have written to me after reading earlier drafts of the chapters on their positions, and I have been helped by their criticisms. Mrs. Miller and I were the guests of Bishop and Mrs. Ramsey, and I benefited from his response to the chapter on his position. The students in my seminars have provided me with criticisms that have helped in this final redrafting of the material. Philip Scharper, Chairman of the Board of the Religious Education Association, put the current version on the right track. My wife, who is always helpful about such things, listened to each chapter as it came out of the typewriter.

I have used translations of the Bible marked as follows:

g—*The Complete Bible: An American Translation*, by J. M. Powis Smith and Edgar J. Goodspeed (copyright 1939 by the University of Chicago Press)

neb—*The New English Bible* (copyright 1961 by the Delegates of the Oxford University Press and the Syndics of the Cambridge University Press)

p—*The New Testament in Modern English*, by J. B. Phillips (copyright 1958 by J. B. Phillips, the Macmillan Co.)

TEV—*Today's English Version of the New Testament* (copyright 1966 by the American Bible Society)

The unmarked scripture quotations are from the *Revised Standard Version of the Bible,* copyrighted 1946 and 1952 by the Division of Christian Education, National Council of Churches.

I am indebted to these and other publishers in cases where they have granted me permission to quote copyrighted material, indicated in the footnotes.

Randolph Crump Miller

Yale University
The Divinity School

THE
LANGUAGE
GAP
AND GOD

I. LANGUAGE AND
THE GOSPELS

"How does one speak of God in a secular age?" This is the complex and difficult question facing all religious teachers and communicators. It is not a new problem, but today it cuts across all areas of religious education. In spite of many developments in educational theory and practice, the evidence of religious illiteracy is startling. In spite of the many people who still attend church school, parochial school, church, and synagogue, the results in terms of articulateness as well as commitment are unsatisfactory.

This stress on the verbal side of education cannot be ignored, although there are many ways of reaching people through appeal to senses other than hearing and seeing, and experiments with multi-media approaches are important. Christianity has historically been a verbal religion, relying on scripture, liturgy, and theology as means of teaching and survival. Life in community, drama in worship, and action in the world have been expressions of Christian living, but at the center has been "the word of God." Much routine teaching has been in terms of using words; it has been linear rather than multi-media; it has been logical and systematic rather than poetic and impressionistic; it has emphasized the givenness of the content rather than the discovery of meaning.

Even in the recent past, an emphasis on the right answer in the catechism, the proper Bible verse, the correct moral decision, or the acceptable behavior in worship has been considered at least a minimal objective for religious education; some teachers have been satisfied with this approach, but others have claimed that such results are a parody of Christian expectations.

Today, however, most teachers are aware that they do not have all the answers. Indeed, some of them are sensitive to the changes taking place in religious thinking, to the uncertainty about many traditional beliefs, and to the difficulty of speaking of God so as to be understood. They are seeking to be honest about their beliefs, to recognize myth and legend and poetry, to see the validity of festival and fantasy, to relate their faith to the secular world, and to speak to the new generation in language that can be understood. These teachers are charged with using a biblical faith as a basis for illuminating today's world, and they are frustrated by the difficulty of interpreting first-century Eastern literature to a twentieth-century technological society.

The language of the early Christians fitted their culture. At first, they used the Jewish scriptures, which reflected the life of the Middle East. As Christianity moved into the world of the Greeks and the Romans, their uses of language changed to meet the new situation. After the canon of the New Testament was closed, they continued with their theologies and later their catechisms to adapt their language to the changing conditions. As long as there was a relatively close connection between the language of Christians and the culture, teaching was not difficult. Even the Reformation with its return to biblical language did not provide too great a strain.

However, whenever Christianity was introduced into a strange culture, difficulties emerged. Missionaries have always faced the problem of how to communicate their beliefs without at the same time introducing their own cultural presuppositions. They usually followed colonial invasions with the cultural accretions that accompanied them. If enough British culture, for example, was introduced in India or Kenya, then the people could become Anglicans at the same time. In countries where Westernizing influences were slight, the missionaries had more difficulty.

When a foreign way of thinking is introduced into a culture, the tendency is to form an antibody to dispel it (as with a transplanted kidney) or to disintegrate as the new form takes over. Unless there is a point of meeting that accepts the merging of the two, the results are disastrous.

A familiar illustration of this point is the failure of the American Indian to be integrated into the common national life. Clyde Kluckhohn spent many years studying the Navahos. He used all the tools of cultural anthropology to observe, classify, and evaluate his data. But he did not understand them. When, finally, he learned to use *their* concepts to describe the facts observed in *their* way, he was confronted with a philosophy that made sense of their way of living. The Navaho view at points is irreconcilable with the white man's, and what seems just and fair to the white man is demoralizing to the Navaho.[1] Every culture and subculture has a system of meanings that identifies it and becomes a basis for the thinking and behavior of its members.

None of us is asking how to think as a Navaho in modern society. The problem is similar, however, if we ask how to be a first-century Jewish-Christian Bible reader, with the accompanying concepts that made sense in that context, in today's world. Or, if this jump seems too big, at least we are asking how we can think as a sixteenth-century follower of Luther, Calvin, Erasmus, or Cranmer in today's world. Or, as the problem seems to

---

[1] See Clyde Kluckhohn, "The Philosophy of the Navaho Indians," F. S. C. Northrop, ed., *Ideological Differences and World Order* (New Haven, Conn.: Yale University Press, 1949), chap. 17; also, F. S. C. Northrop, *Man, Nature and God* (New York: Pocket Books, Inc., 1962), pp. 34–35.

emerge today, how one who thinks in terms of the Christian beliefs of the 1950's can be relevant in the world of the youth of the 1970's with their own subculture, of those who are developing a new sense of identity in the black subculture, or of the members of a technological society that has lost the sense of mystery and poetry.

This problem has become clearer as we approach new studies in religious language. Ian T. Ramsey suggests that when we see that

> these biblical narratives and classical references were themselves interlocked with a contemporary culture and social pattern, and in this wider context had their point, then there is reason to hope that this original point may now break in on us as we bring alongside our own particular situation. We may then, using an obvious model, talk of God speaking to us in our own day.[2]

Ramsey's diagnosis is probably correct, but the solution bristles with difficulties. Our Western culture has moved so rapidly in the past half century, our ways of thinking have been so affected by the scientific, technological, and secular advances, that our situation seems divorced almost completely from society as presupposed in biblical and traditional theological thinking. Achievements in terms of comfortable living, rapid transportation, mass media, and health turn people's thoughts to technology, automation, and computers. The increasing urbanization, with its attendant problems, leaves little room for meditating on rural and nomadic scenes in biblical literature. Social changes, especially as demanded by blacks and students, point to new idealisms and new pressures. Poetry, mystery, and talk about revelation have more and more dropped out of contemporary life. Traditional moral sanctions are seriously questioned.

Biblical language might free us from some of these limitations if we were capable of thinking in such images, but we have

----

[2] Ian T. Ramsey, *On Being Sure in Religion* (London: The Athlone Press, 1963), p. 35.

become too literal in our thinking. Are we not like Nicodemus who, when Jesus talked about being reborn, wanted to know if one would literally return to his mother's womb? What do we do with such phrases as "Christ lives in me" or "work out your own salvation. . . . but Christ works in you" or (from Ignatius of Antioch) "Jesus Christ, his son, who is his word proceeding from silence"? Christianity formed its own vivid, imageful, poetic vocabulary, and the question today is, What does it all mean?

CHRISTIANITY A SPEECH-EVENT

As background for any approach to Christian education through the insights of the findings of the philosophers of language, we need to look closely at the uses of language in the Bible, and especially in the Gospels. Amos N. Wilder provides an analysis of early Christian uses of language which is extremely helpful.[3] It is the nontechnical speech of the common man, lacking in literary pretensions. It is a language with uplifting properties, speaking of new tongues and new songs, reporting on events and teachings that promise the coming of salvation. Because it was a new way of looking at God, man, and the world, it needed new forms of expression.

Ernst Fuchs has called Christianity a "speech-event," a renewal of myth. "Primitive Christianity," he writes, "is itself a speech phenomenon. It is for this very reason that it established a monument in the new style-form which we call a 'gospel.' The Johannine Apocalypse and, indeed, in the first instance the apostolic epistle-literature, these are creations of a new utterance which changes everything it touches."[4]

The religion of Israel, even though it appealed to all the

---

[3] Amos N. Wilder, *The Language of the Gospels: Early Christian Rhetoric* (New York: Harper & Row, 1964). This book provides the basis for many of the comments in this chapter.

[4] Ernst Fuchs, "Die Sprache im Neuen Testament," *Zur Frage nach dem historischen Jesus* (Tübingen, 1960), p. 261; quoted by Wilder, op. cit., p. 18.

senses, had a special place for hearing, and as the oral mode became permanent, it was transferred to the written. It was not a scientific and descriptive language but a means of providing God's commands for the hearers who are expected to respond. Thus Israel and after it Christianity became religions of the "book."

There was no holy language; it was the common everyday language translated into whatever tongue the listeners spoke and infused with the enthusiasm of the believers. The New Testament used the rich store of images in the Old Testament, interpreting them with great freedom and mixing them with new ones. Only occasionally were Old Testament prophecies used in a wooden way to underscore the significance of an act of Jesus.

The oral speech behind the written record seemed often to be extempore and immediately relevant. This was particularly true of the words of Jesus, whose use of direct discourse and dialogue led to confrontation not only with him but through him with the Father. Paul preferred oral speech and sent letters as a substitute, and even these letters preserved the occasional nature of spoken dialogue.

Even though Christianity placed great emphasis on the word, and especially the oral word, it was not "just talk." The purpose was to portray a revelation and not to win an argument. Therefore, the writings were brief and to the point. One makes a different selection of points to bring about a new insight from those chosen to win a debate. The Gospels, written to reveal the nature of the Son of God, do not pretend to be biographies of Jesus. No inflated rhetoric was necessary, and the need for brevity led to both liberation and purification in the use of language.

Two other points made by Wilder need to be kept in mind. First, the significance and depth of the New Testament writings were "evidently deeply determined by the faith or life-orientation that produced them." [5] Second, particular social patterns led to the formation of this literature, which is the ex-

---

[5] Wilder, op. cit., p. 34.

pression of the faith of a community. A new society had been formed which used these materials in their worship and in their common life, and in turn these demands forged the materials prior to their final written form.

These new forms cannot be identified simply as history, biography, oratory, or poetry, although these are elements in the writings. Partly because Christianity was a novelty in its own right and was a "speech-event," and partly because it arose out of a tradition of Judaism and the Orient, these categories do not fit. Wilder suggests that we use Gospel, dialogue, story, parable, poem, and myth.

GOSPEL

The one new kind of writing is the Gospel. It does not fit the categories of biography, hero story, or tragedy. It is not a myth or saga. It is not the work of a single author. It is a community's expression of the record of "a divine transaction whose import involves heaven and earth" [6] in which the believer finds himself a participant. Here is the meaning of life for the believer in community, as he himself is transformed into a new being.

Yet the four Gospels are not alike. Mark is something of a faith story. Matthew is more a tract of instruction. Luke–Acts is written as if from a later perspective. John is more like a "sacred drama or oratorio." The major thrust of these writings is found in microcosm in the anecdotes of healing and exorcism, in the parables, and in the passion and resurrection stories as the "concrete dramatization of the power of God effecting what is impossible with men." [7]

The Gospels combine what Jesus said and did with the faith of the Christian community, and this community knew Jesus partly by remembrance but chiefly as a living, contemporary, and human-divine figure who needed to be interpreted in order that the community could live in terms of its divine com-

---

[6] Ibid., pp. 36–37.
[7] Ibid., pp. 37–38.

mission. It not only needed to hear the Gospel; it also needed to weave the Gospel into its worship and life. The earliest liturgical forms grew from the soul of the Gospels; the earliest preaching recounted the Gospel anecdotes or summarized the whole story as did Peter at Pentecost. For a time this process was chiefly oral, partly because oral transmission was customary but chiefly because oral transmission provided the sense of immediacy that the Gospels intended. The expectation that God would bring an end to things made written words unnecessary. Even when the expectation of the end was postponed, the immediacy of the claim of God upon them was never lost. This note of immediacy remains today as an essential note of the Gospels.

It is not hard to believe that the early followers of Christ found this kind of reality in the Gospels. But the twentieth-century Western man has difficulty today in recreating the sense of urgency. Man has his own anxieties in the twentieth century, which may be as pressing as those of the first century, but he has difficulty in grasping the meaning of his life in terms of the Gospel. The Gospel as a "speech-event" forces modern educators to look to the analysis of language to discover how the basic meaning of the Gospel can be communicated in today's world.

Epistles

There is nothing new about the letter form, and in the days of the New Testament letters were sometimes unsigned or written in another's name. Discourses meant for wide circulation were sometimes written as letters. The value of a letter is that it is personal and flexible and comes nearest to oral speech. Some of Paul's letters were dictated and maintain an oral atmosphere. Letters, furthermore, can be relevant to a particular situation and may become part of a dialogue.

What is radically new about Paul's letters is the way in which they are addressed, an opening which is Christianized and which presents the writer as one who speaks under God for the community. They serve a purpose different from that of the

Gospels. They are more didactic, include some dogmatic statements, provide moral instruction, and even suggest forms of organization. Beneath these practical considerations, they express in ways that often approach poetry the deepest aspects of Christian faith. They seek to express in new ways the mystery of the transaction whereby Jesus Christ mediates salvation to those who believe.

Take, for example, Paul's statement in 2 Corinthians 6:8–10: "As deceivers, yet true; as unknown, and yet well known; as dying, and behold, we live; as chastened, and not killed; as sorrowful, yet always rejoicing; as poor, yet making many rich; as having nothing, yet possessing all things." This passage has been full of vivacity and power for many believers, as it was for Paul's original readers. Yet, if it is reduced to a logical definition, it is absurd. "A theological paradox," writes Charles Hartshorne, "it appears, is what a contradiction becomes when it is about God rather than something else, or indulged in by a theologian or a church rather than an unbeliever or a heretic." [8] However, the canons of logic may not be suitable for judging this statement; for this assertion, just because of its logical oddity or paradoxical form, may trigger a disclosure that is essential to the possibility of a religious commitment.

We may use the epistles, then, for a variety of purposes. As occasional letters, they sought to speak to specific situations, and each situation required its own content and logic. Only on occasion did Paul's imagination rise to flights of paradox and poetic forms. This is where the high poetry of the passage on love in 1 Corinthians 13 or the paradoxes on the nature of sin in Romans 7 have immediate cash value. A careful analysis of the use and meaning of his language is essential for using his writings today.

We may come to the same conclusions concerning the letters which are not so direct and personal in intent (e.g., James)

<hr>

[8] Charles Hartshorne, *The Divine Relativity: A Social Conception of God* (New Haven, Conn.: Yale University Press, 1948), p. 1.

and examine them on their own terms. These letters show more concern with the language of obligation as it is related to the language of faith. To be equipped for ministry in the world becomes an essential part of the educational process.

DIALOGUE

The preference for the oral as against the written tradition continued even after the New Testament was in written form. Quotations from the early Church Fathers often are variations of the written form and represent what they heard. Wilder believes that we now have tools for getting closer to the oral forms, for they also had their own conventions. "The perennial features of natural eloquence had been developed to a high art in the tradition that lay behind the parables and aphorisms of Jesus." [9] We find a combination of novelty and tradition so that images and forms were affected by the content.

There is much two-way speech in the Gospels: dialogue in the forms of question and answer, discussion, and story and comment. We see the background for this in the Old Testament, especially in God's dealings with men, where men listen to God, argue with him, and submit to him. There are also many passages of dialogue between men. In the New Testament, this tradition is carried on.

The power of such dialogue is illustrated by the denial of Peter when he was accused of being with Jesus prior to Jesus' arrest: "I do not know this man of whom you speak (Mark 14:71)." Wilder says:

> We have here a plebian, low-life episode involving personalities that are nonentities—a police court disturbance. Yet in our gospel context all the issues of world-history gather about it; issues of blessedness and damnation, whether for Peter, or for those to whom the early message was orally preached, or for us who read it after two millennia. This new plain rhetoric of the Gospel was what it was only because it was prompted by a new direct speech or word of God himself to men. What

9 Wilder, op. cit., p. 51.

makes such stories and such dialogue so formidable is that in each one God, as it were, forces us to give him a face-to-face answer, or, to look him in the eye.[10]

It is an illuminating experience to go through the Gospels seeking to identify genuine dialogue. Sometimes the questions are staged or inept, as so often in the Fourth Gospel, but there is a realism about most of the situations in which "radical personal challenge and encounter are primary." [11] To discover who puts the question or what the situation is, to see the force of the answers or the point of the discussion, is to be drawn into the significance of the dialogue ourselves. This may be carried over into the responses in worship, antiphonal forms of prayer, and hearing the sermon.

The use of dialogue has become dominant in some theories of Christian education in recent years. Reuel L. Howe has defined it as "that address and response between persons in which there is a flow of meaning between them in spite of all the obstacles that normally would block the relationship." [12]

If we take a more verbal view of dialogue, as do the linguistic philosophers, we need to be sure of the agreed meaning and uses of the words. Jesus is portrayed in dialogue with enemies who have not sought an interpersonal relationship with him. Their questions are meant to trap him into indiscreet or treasonous replies. He needs to understand the implications as well as the direct meaning of their questions and to answer in a way that will safeguard his meaning. But in his discourses with his disciples, Jesus is portrayed as having a sound interpersonal relationship and yet the disciples have difficulty in understanding what seems to us, from our standpoint, as the plain meaning of his replies.

One purpose of dialogue is to get people on the same wave-

---

[10] Ibid., p. 56.

[11] Ibid., p. 61.

[12] Reuel L. Howe, *The Miracle of Dialogue* (New York: Seabury Press, 1962), p. 37.

length, to establish the way words are being used, to agree on which language-game is valid for the particular purpose. For example, when a seven-year-old asks, "Is it true?" his language is that of the one who wants to test the assertion by an appeal to experience; he is uninterested in more sophisticated theories of the nature of truth, and he considers myths, fairy tales, legends, parables, and poetry to be "untrue" even if useful. But the dialogue does not clarify anything unless we can operate in terms of his view of truth, which establishes the form of his language-game. The problem is similar when a child asks, "Which came first, Adam and Eve or the dinosaur?" He has already mixed his language-games and it is necessary to establish the proper categories of language before either Adam and Eve or extinct Mesozoic Saurian reptiles can profitably be discussed. The dinosaur belongs properly to the scientific language of the reconstruction of biological history, and the Genesis story belongs to a biblical category of mythic thinking. The proper use of question and answer can help the student to make distinctions on his own, and the art of conversation is an excellent tool for eliminating misconceptions based on category mistakes.

A final point about dialogue is that it can be a means of insight when the answer is unexpected or contains an element of distortion or hyperbole. This is evident in much of the dialogue given to us in the Gospels. A mixing of logically odd assertions from two language-games may lead to a disclosure. A statement, "Thou art the man," can convict David of his misdeed with Bathsheba.

STORIES

Another important literary form in the Gospels is the story. Teachers have always used stories, often with certain aids to memorization such as rhythms, factual expressions, and gestures. Stories are living, oral speech.

The Gospel stories have some unique characteristics, according to Wilder. They have a simple, secular base that may be misleading, for they point beyond the immediate experience.

They draw into themselves the great plot of God's redemption of mankind, reflecting the overall drama of the Bible in many small subplots. They have a power to draw the listener into the meaning of the story. "Perhaps the special character of the stories in the New Testament lies in the fact that they are not told for themselves, that they are not only about other people, but that they are always about us." [13] The story may end, but our participation may carry on in terms of challenge, belief, and action.

One impression we get from the Gospels is that they are strung together from a number of anecdotes which are not necessarily in the order in which they occurred, even if they are historical. They probably circulated as independent units at first; they were sharpened and improved with constant retelling, although some may have been garnished with extra details and therefore became less clearly focused. Undoubtedly some were dropped from the repertoire, as the Gospel of John suggests. These anecdotes were fitted into the larger frame of reference, usually from the perspective of the post-Easter church.

Because of the post-resurrection viewpoint, anecdotes of healing and exorcism were combined with the passion story and the words of Jesus as the Son of God in a transaction that changed heaven and earth. The faith of the community was expressed by and undergirded by the Gospels.

Wilder illustrates this thesis with one of the healing stories.[14] We miss the point if we concentrate on Jesus the wonder worker or use the story to bolster our hopes when we go to a healing service or shrine. These things may or may not be suitable, but they are not the point of the story. The meaning of the event is seen in a post-resurrection perspective "as a manifestation of a general redemption for the whole people of God." Physical, moral, and spiritual distress were all one for the early Christians, and they were concerned with the redemption of the total person.

---

[13] Wilder, op. cit., p. 65.
[14] See ibid., pp. 70–74.

The place of the story in Christian education is of paramount significance, and we will return to this topic from time to time. A special form of it is the parable.

PARABLES

The parables are integral parts of the telling of the story of redemption. They have great variety of form but always speak of the purpose of revelation. They are more like a metaphor than a simile, for a metaphor provides "an image with a certain shock to the imagination which directly conveys vision of what is signified." [15] A metaphor, as Ian T. Ramsey says, "yields many possibilities of articulation," [16] and this opens up the variety of interpretations some parables have received. Some scholars insist that a parable has only a single point, and to find other points is like pushing an analogy too far. Yet both Wilder and Ramsey assert that a metaphor, like a parable, stimulates the imagination and therefore evokes insight that it may not control.

Jesus' parables reflect the places and times of his own ministry. They have a secular note about them. There may be some Old Testament allusions, which are also secular. As a result, the moral and religious applications or implications refer to the world in which men live. There is no precious religiosity in them.

Wilder helps our understanding of the parables of the kingdom. Because they are clearly metaphorical, they stimulate the imagination in various ways, and so, from Wilder's point of

---

[15] Ibid., p. 80.

[16] Ian T. Ramsey, *Models and Mystery* (London: Oxford University Press, 1964), p. 48. See his whole treatment of the topic, pp. 48–57. "A simile is a comparison proclaimed as such, whereas a metaphor is a tacit comparison made by the substitution of the compared notion for the one to be illustrated. . . . Every metaphor presupposes a simile & every simile is compressible or convertible into a metaphor. . . . It may fairly be said that every parable is extended metaphor & allegory extended simile." Margaret Nicholson, *A Dictionary of American-English Usage*, based on Fowler's *Modern English Usage* (New York: Oxford University Press, 1957), p. 520.

view, they may be misinterpreted as, say, parables of growth. They need a context in which the harvest is coming. The prophetic expectation is to be fulfilled in the here and now. Jesus combined the language of the coming kingdom and the language of the layman to make his point. He is not advising the farmer to "keep his chin up" because next year the rains might come. "The kingdom of heaven is like treasure hidden in a field, which a man found and covered up; then in his joy he goes and sells all that he has and buys the field (Matt. 13:44)." Here the emphasis is on "the joy in the discovery" and not on the value or the sacrifice.[17]

Both parables and stories are essential in all teaching. The language philosophers, as we shall see, are happy with both, especially with the parable because it is never purely factual and therefore needs no verification. Yet a parable has a basic realism about it, which can be destroyed if it becomes too obviously allegorical. Perhaps this is the proper test for all parables: if the ornamentation is not necessary for the parable to make its points, then that portion of it should be eliminated. Jesus' parables stand up under this test. Those who are teachers necessarily tell their own parables, and the penetrating realism of Jesus is a proper example of what teachers in their lesser ways are trying to do.

POETRY

The poetry of the Bible, and especially of the Gospels, does not fit into our Western norms, except that rhythm is basic. In the New Testament, the poetic prose of the Greeks and the parallelism and accentuated rhythms of the Jews are apparent. We find aphorisms, prophetic oracles, psalms, and hymns, some of which reflect heathen patterns with a Jewish or Christian cast.[18] It is not easy for the modern Western mind to distin-

---

[17] Wilder, op. cit., p. 94.
[18] See ibid., pp. 103–5, 112; also Ian T. Ramsey, *Christian Discourse* (London: Oxford University Press, 1965), pp. 14–20.

guish prose from poetry, and one is not helped by the way many translations of the Bible have been printed.[19]

The early Christian community had its own poetry and songs: "Let the word of Christ dwell in you richly, as you teach and admonish one another in all wisdom, and as you sing psalms and hymns and spiritual songs with thankfulness in your hearts to God (Col. 3:16)." The freedom and creativity of the speech-event are evident, especially when we remember that speaking with tongues expressed this same enthusiasm. Such poetry was naive and lacking in sophistication and sustained style, but it sang a new song in no uncertain tones.

As we will see in chapter 6, this use of what Canon Drinkwater calls "poetic-simple" language is significant for the communication of religious faith. It is the language of disclosure, discernment, or insight; and its proper use may evoke a new way of looking on life. It is a language-game in a new dimension, and it has its own uses and meanings which point to a reality that includes a profound mystery, the mystery of life and death.

MYTH

Western categories do not take adequate account of myth. Myth, ritual, and emotion interact in primitive religion, and they are necessary in any profound worship. This "mythic mentality" runs throughout the New Testament. Such pictorial imagery reaches a surrealist stage in the Book of Revelation, but this must not hinder us from seeing how mythic thinking permeates all the writings.

Wilder understands myth

> in the sense of total world-representation, involving, of course, not only what we would call the external cosmos but man as well, and all in the light of God. . . . If the Word of God must necessarily speak with the mythopoetic words of men, it

---

[19] See, for examples, Ephesians 5:4; 1 Timothy 3:16; 2 Timothy 2:11a–13a; 1 John 2:9–11.

is all the more inevitable that this should be so where the ultimate issues of existence are in question.[20]

We are operating here with a specialized language-game, a category of language that cannot be reduced to factual description, and yet with imagery that cannot be reproduced without assistance in the twentieth century. The early Christians formulated the myths of their time both to express their faith and to combat early or erroneous contemporary myths. Just as twentieth-century myths have to be combatted, so did earlier ones. We have had Hitler's myth of Aryan superiority and the place of the Jews, myths that accept scientism as an accurate portrayal of the meaning of life, myths of the destiny of the American nation as a melting pot or as a guardian of the world, and the myth of Horatio Alger. But we have difficulties with the myths of the New Testament, and we need to learn how to use mythopoetic language derived from the biblical faith in the modern world. To this problem we will return in chapter 4.

EDUCATIONAL IMPLICATIONS

What this chapter has demonstrated is that insofar as Christian education is based on the Bible we have to see how much we rely on specific literary forms for teaching. These forms are sometimes alien to the modern generation, or at least they are not recognized as the forms being used and therefore the wrong questions are asked of them. Any mixture of categories of language can be dangerous, and yet some mixing is essential if one is to gain insight into religious meanings. Further analysis of religious language is necessary if we are to clarify our verbal approaches to teaching.

But even as we begin this study, we can gain some educational insights from Wilder's approach as it stands. He warns that "one cannot merely repeat the words of the Bible, or lay one passage of the New Testament next to another, and so pre-

---

[20] Wilder, op. cit., pp. 128–29. A consideration of Bultmann's approach to myth appears in chapter 4.

tend to communicate the gospel." [21] Interpretation is essential. We need to discover what the images meant originally, within the life situation of the speaker and the hearers, and this opens up the possibility of interpretation for our own day.

Wilder, like others whom we will examine, places emphasis on the story, for it is through the story that the Christian confesses his faith. Personages in stories can be identified with, and thus the purposes of the stories may be appropriated. In this sense, every Christian story is open-ended, leaving the future in the hands of the hearers. Furthermore, when enough stories have been told, the hearer begins to see the framework of the Christian view of life, with its emphasis on the work of God in the world and on the promise of salvation. Every form of Christian rhetoric derives ultimately from this world view.

Another implication is that the teacher must be able to move from theological to lay language. This is what parables are admirably equipped to do. To do this takes a combination of imagination, sensitivity, and skills that challenge any teacher.

However, the Bible remains a strange book. The more prosaic minds have not been happy with it, and some of the philosophers of language, in spite of their use of stories, have difficulty with the rich, mythic, paradoxical imagery. The daring assertions about the nature of God, Jesus Christ, the Holy Spirit, man, and the world strain the credulity of the modern man. He finds the following statement made by Horace Bushnell in 1849 difficult to accept:

> There is no book in the world that contains so many repugnances, or antagonistic forms of assertion, as the Bible. Therefore, if any man please to play off his constructive logic upon it, he can easily show it up as the absurdest book in the world. But whoever wants, on the other hand, really to behold and receive all truth, and would have the truth-world overhang him as an empyrean of stars, complex, multitudinous, striving antagonistically, yet comprehended, height above height, and deep under deep, in a boundless score of harmony; what man

---

[21] Ibid., p. 130.

soever, content with no small rote of logic and catechism, reaches with true hunger after this, and will offer himself to the many-sided forms of the scripture with a perfectly ingenuous and receptive spirit; he shall find his nature flooded with senses, vastnesses, and powers of truth, such as it is even greatness to feel.[22]

Bushnell's statement is fundamentally sound, especially when it is understood within the context of his theory of religious language, which we will consider in chapter 6, but it may mislead those who are caught up in some forms of biblical theology. Biblical theology has been helpful in clarifying some of the major themes of the Bible and in seeing that it has a complex unity. It is necessary that we think of the Bible as a record of the mighty acts of God, and it may well be understood as a drama, the five acts being Creation, Covenant, Christ, Church, Consummation.[23] But within this drama, each portion of scripture must be examined on its own merits or it may be twisted out of its proper context in order to fit a prearranged scheme. Furthermore, there is no excuse to move beyond proper linguistic analysis in considering the meaning of terms.

It is at this point that James Barr's warnings are relevant. There is a school of thought that advises us to "think biblically," and yet neglects "the social consciousness of the meaning of words," and "the exact contribution made by a word in its context and communicated between the speaker and the hearer, or the writer and the reader." [24] They have their good words and their bad words, and they seek to fit their biblical materials into a "good word" theology. The objection, from the standpoint of language analysis, is that they have not paid ade-

---

[22] Horace Bushnell, *God in Christ* (Hartford: Parsons & Brown, 1849), pp. 69–70; reprinted in H. Shelton Smith, ed., *Horace Bushnell* (New York and London: Oxford University Press, 1965), pp. 96–97.

[23] See my *Biblical Theology and Christian Education* (New York: Charles Scribner's Sons, 1956).

[24] James Barr, *Semantics of Biblical Language* (London: Oxford University Press, 1961), p. 281.

quate attention to the normal use and meaning of words. If the Bible is to speak plainly, it must not be subject to imposed patterns even if they seem to be theologically proper.

Wilder's approach avoids this kind of distortion, and if we follow his approach in Christian education we will be on the right track. Within the broad scope of belief in a "God who acts," we are free to examine the speech and actions of men, and we discover that most of their language is nonspecialized and nontechnical, with occasional words that are specifically religious in their connotation. The ease with which the early Christians translated their writings into Greek and other languages indicates that they, at least, had no prejudice in favor of any language, even Hebrew or Aramaic, for communicating religious ideas. In Christian education, then, the translation that comes closest to being the language of the students is the one to use.

Yet this early Christian vocabulary was plastic, rich, poetic, logically odd, and in some cases novel. In our effort to show that there was no "holy language," we must not forget that the language dealt with such concepts as "holy," "glory," and visions of the future, and did so in such a way that enduring impressions were made on the total persons of those who came under its influence.

As we turn to consider the theories of religious language that can help us in the proper verbal uses in Christian education, we need to keep in mind that the "God-talk" of the early Christians was on the whole nonspecialized and secular, and yet such talk dealt with holy things and with the drama of the salvation of mankind.

II. THE CHALLENGE OF LANGUAGE ANALYSIS

The use of words and sentences derived from the Bible as a basis for Christian education has led to more and more difficulties in the modern world. When one adds to the Bible such forms as catechisms, theological propositions, literary sources not based on the Bible, and the normal discourse of teaching situations, it is clear that the results are less than satisfactory.

We have chosen to explore the findings of contemporary language analysis as one way of mapping, however roughly, the logical placing of the language of faith. Linguistic analysis is a use of philosophical tools to get at the verification, use, and meaning of words in their contexts. We take religious assertions, examine their functions, check the possibilities of testing them in experience, and come to conclusions about the meaning that may be communicated.

Such a study should prove valuable for anyone involved in the communication of Christian beliefs, especially teachers of religion in churches and schools but also those who participate in the educational process at every level. Some of the findings, being primarily negative, can serve only as a warning to those with minds that tend to literal interpretations of religious language. More recent findings, however, point to more creative and imaginative uses of religious assertions that move beyond an empirical base.

EARLY LINGUISTIC ANALYSIS

A new tool was introduced into philosophy in the late 1920's. A group of scientifically trained philosophers meeting in Vienna began asking about the proper use of language, beginning with a minimum of propositions. At this early stage, the movement had no place for religious or metaphysical propositions, and there was no direct contribution to Christian education. But we need to understand why this was so, both because the warnings were important and because of the development of this movement of analysis to the point at which it is extremely valuable to the building of a theory of Christian education.

Is it meaningful to talk about God at all? In the early days of linguistic analysis the answer was an unqualified "No!" The key issue turned on the verification principle. A logical analysis of the use and meaning of words, it was said, led to two types of language: (1) tautologies, where what is said is logically true, as in mathematics or in such statements as "a rose is a rose" or "I am I," and (2) synthetic or nonanalytic sentences, in which the meaning is its method of verification. For example, if one says, "It is raining outside," the listener can look outside and see it or go outside and get wet. The way in which even a scientific formula makes sense to a layman is to reduce it to the tests which verified it. Thus, only sentences which can be verified in sense experience have validity.

Now it is obvious that many sentences do not fit these two categories, but for the early linguistic analysts no other kinds make sense. If a sentence cannot be tested in sense experience, it is said to have "emotive" meaning but it is literally "nonsense." All poetry, religious and metaphysical thinking, and ethical principles fall into this category, and therefore cannot be called true assertions. This was the extreme position, and it became popular among a small number of philosophers. However, it reflected one kind of scientific mentality and can be found among many people who would not be able to expound it.

This point of view was popularized by A. J. Ayer. He modified the position slightly by making room for *probable* knowledge based on history, provided it was tested in someone else's experience, calling this "weak" verification. He still dismissed all ethical, metaphysical, and religious statements as having no meaning except to make people feel good. "We often say that the nature of God is a mystery which transcends the human understanding. But to say that something transcends the human understanding is to say that it is unintelligible. And what is unintelligible cannot be significantly described." He was equally condemnatory of the mystic with his visions of God, who, "so far from producing propositions that are empirically verifiable, is unable to produce any intelligible propositions at all." [1] Ayer was perfectly willing to agree that a person who *thought* he was experiencing God had experienced a certain kind of sense content, but this does not lead to the verification of a statement about a transcendent God.

The other side of the coin, which seems to some people to be equally devastating, is the principle of falsifiability. If someone believes in God, say, on the evidence of experience or tradition, what kind of evidence would falsify this belief? How much evil in the world would cause a believer to cease to believe? The believer makes vast assertions about the power and goodness of God which seem to be factual, and then he begins to qualify them, until finally, as Antony Flew put it, the belief dies a "death by a thousand qualifications." "Now an assertion, to be an assertion at all, must claim that things stand thus and thus; *and not otherwise.* Similarly an explanation, to be an explanation, must explain why this particular thing occurs; *and not something else.* Those last clauses are crucial." [2] Many religious

[1] A. J. Ayer, *Language, Truth, and Logic* (2d ed.; London: Gollancz, 1936), p. 118.

[2] Antony Flew and Alasdair MacIntyre, eds., *New Essays in Philosophical Theology* (London: SCM Press, 1955), p. 106; see also Antony

thinkers, says Flew, try to hold to two conclusions at once, either as a paradox or as an unrecognized contradiction, and this is a form of *doublethink* as described by George Orwell: " '*Doublethink* means the power of holding two contradictory beliefs simultaneously, and accepting both of them. The party intellectual knows that he is playing tricks with reality, but by the exercise of *doublethink* he also satisfies himself that reality is not violated.' " [3]

There is no easy way to resolve such contradictions. One answer is that we "know by faith." But if the belief is contradictory or incomprehensible, it is not clear what is being believed whether by faith or otherwise. "If you do not know what it is you are believing on faith," asks Bernard Williams, "how can you be sure that you are believing anything?" [4]

Thomas McPherson, in a cryptic statement, summarizes this point of view: "What to the Jews was a stumbling-block and to the Greeks foolishness is to the logical positivists nonsense." He takes seriously the reports of mystical experience as the experience of the inexpressible and agrees that what is essential in religious beliefs cannot be put into words. Therefore, "the way out of the worry is to retreat into silence." [5] McPherson claims to be a friend of religion but an enemy of theology, because "religion belongs to the sphere of the unutterable." By "nonsense" he means what is not verifiable by sense experience. He places Rudolf Otto, Ludwig Wittgenstein, and Martin Buber in the same category and suggests that the "I–Thou relation" vanishes when one tries to analyze it, because it then becomes "I–It." [6] Or as Martin Buber put it: "A God *about* whom one can talk is not a God *to* whom one can pray." [7]

Flew, *God and Philosophy* (New York: Harcourt, Brace & World, 1966) for a full-fledged attack on belief in God.

   [3] *1984*, p. 220; quoted in Flew and MacIntyre, op. cit., p. 108.

   [4] Ibid., p. 209.

   [5] Ibid., p. 133–34.

   [6] Ibid., p. 141, n.

   [7] As quoted by Heinrich Ott and reported by Dietrich Ritschl, *Memory and Hope* (New York: Macmillan, 1967), p. 158, n.

The results so far are primarily negative. They seem to leave Christian education with nothing to do except perhaps to provide the opportunity (in silent worship?) for an experience (hopefully) of the holy. What these findings serve to do, however, is to be a warning to all teachers that pupils who have been trained in strictly critical scientific thinking may want to apply the categories of literal sense experience to religious beliefs, with similar negative results. If they do this, one cannot get out of such a situation by the application of *doublethink*, appeals to knowing "by faith," or even by relying on tradition as authority. We will return to these issues in chapter 3.

FUNCTIONAL ANALYSIS

The reliance on strict rules of verification, however, was seen by the philosophers of language to be so limiting that very little was left to talk about. Language simply is not used in this limited way. It is obvious that many sentences function in such a way that meanings are communicated, although such meanings cannot be equated with a hard-nosed empiricism. Wittgenstein saw this clearly when he listed many possible language-games, by which he meant that there are different levels or orders or categories of use of language in which sentences find their meaning in their use. He listed some of them as follows:

Review the multiplicity of language-games in the following examples, and in others:

Giving orders, and obeying them—
Describing the appearance of an object, or giving its measurements—
Constructing an object from a description (a drawing)—
Reporting an event—
Speculating about an event—
Forming and resting a hypothesis—
Presenting the results of an experiment in tables and diagrams—
Making up a story; and reading it—
Play-acting—

Singing catches—
Guessing riddles—
Making a joke; telling it—
Solving a problem in practical arithmetic—
Translating from one language to another—
Asking, thanking, cursing, greeting, praying—

—It is interesting to compare the multiplicity of the tools in language and of the ways they are used, the multiplicity of the kinds of word and sentence, with what logicians have said about the structure of language. (Including the author of the *Tractatus Logico-Philosophicus.*) [8]

The concept of language-game is not frivolous, and it may prove of profound importance in the communication of religious assertions. It indicates that there are different uses of language according to sets of rules. Just as cricket and basketball have little in common besides having their own rules, so language-games have sharp differences. But there are families of language-games just as softball, Little League baseball, and professional baseball have similar rules with a few significant differences. But this does not mean that you can play checkers while I play contract bridge, and that we will have no dealings with each other.

The danger is that someone will want to play solitaire and claim that his game is the only legitimate one, so that all words and sentences are used with arbitrary and artificial meanings. Or, on the other hand, someone will claim that he has a game that includes all the others, just as the Olympic Games Committee controls all the sporting events at the Olympics. But track and swimming and sailing remain different games, and this is where the players are.[9]

---

[8] Ludwig Wittgenstein, *Philosophical Investigations* (2d ed.; Oxford: Basil Blackwell, 1958; New York: Macmillan, 1958), pp. 11e–12e.

[9] See ibid., pp. 31e–32e; William Hordern, *Speaking of God* (New York: Macmillan, 1964), p. 87; James A. Martin, Jr., *The New Dialogue Between Philosophy and Theology* (New York: Seabury Press, 1966), pp. 108–9, 154–60.

"The term 'language-*game*' is meant to bring into prominence the fact that the speaking of language is part of an activity, or of a form of life," says Wittgenstein.[10] The human form of life stands behind all language. There is no higher order of language than that provided by human beings who are both responsible and responsive. A person backs his language by his life *as a whole*, and yet he participates in many language-games.[11] It may be, then, that as a religious person speaks, he uses language that reflects the meaning to be found in his own life style.

The meaning of a word or a sentence is found in its use rather than in its testing. Analysis is used to uncover misuses and to clarify actual uses. The use of a word in one sentence can be compared with its use in another in which its meaning is admittedly clear. Key words used religiously, if the meaning is not immediately clear in our modern culture, can be placed in their ordinary secular setting in order to clarify the meaning. For example, when "redemption" is discussed in a religious setting, its meaning may be clarified by using the word in relation to the redemption of bonds or of stamps at a "Green Stamp Redemption Center." When its crasser meaning has become clear, it may be possible to transfer its use back to its religious significance, possibly with adequate limiting qualifiers.

A variation of this principle of meaning according to use is modified by R. B. Braithwaite. He takes seriously the claim that we cannot verify statements about God, thus eliminating this issue from the discussion, and moves directly to the use of religious assertions for moral purposes. "A statement," he says, "need not itself be empirically verifiable, but that it is used in a particular way is always a straightforwardly empirical proposition." [12] By using "empirical" in this way, he lets ethics into the

---

[10] Wittgenstein, op. cit., p. 11e.

[11] See Dallas M. High, *Language, Persons, and Belief* (New York: Oxford University Press, 1967), pp. 99–106.

[12] *An Empiricist's View of the Nature of Religious Belief* (Cambridge: Cambridge University Press, 1955), p. 11.

discussion, but he has already applied a more stringent empirical test for the word God. What he has done is to reduce all meaningful religious assertions to moral statements, so that one may "follow an agapeistic way of life," [13] which is the way of love.

The purpose of religious teaching is served by telling stories that encourage Christian love. The purpose of a story is to strengthen one's resolutions to follow a way of life, and different religions have different stories. It is irrelevant whether the stories are true, and this irrelevance is considered important. Braithwaite writes:

> My contention that the propositional element in religious assertions consists of stories interpreted as straightforwardly empirical propositions which are not, generally speaking, believed to be true has the great advantage of imposing no restriction whatever upon the empirical interpretation which can be put upon the stories. The religious man may interpret the stories in the way which assists him best in carrying out the behavior policies of his religion.[14]

On Braithwaite's grounds, the teacher could select any story that serves to strengthen moral intentions.

It is easy to demonstrate that such stories, with no basis in fact, do serve this purpose. Jesus told parables that have had profound effects on men's behavior, without there being such a person as a good Samaritan, a wicked steward, or a prodigal son. Children have been nurtured on stories from secular sources, from Aesop's Fables to Batman, which have had moral implications. But there is more to Christian education than this.

THE EASTER EVENT

The most serious and consistent attempt to deal with the Christian story from the point of view of verification of asser-

---

[13] Ibid., p. 19.

[14] Ibid., p. 29. See Ian T. Ramsey, ed., *Christian Ethics and Contemporary Philosophy* (London: SCM Press, 1966), pp. 74–94, for comments on Braithwaite's position and Braithwaite's response.

tions about God and Jesus is that of Paul M. van Buren. "Christian faith," he writes, "has to do with the New Testament witness to Jesus of Nazareth and what took place in his history. Christology, however it may be interpreted, will lie at the center of our understanding of the gospel." [15]

The difficulty with talk about God, says van Buren, is that the word does not refer to anything that can be described in empirical language. All statements about God can be translated into statements about man without losing their meaning. Today, we do not know enough to say that "God is dead," but it is certain that "the *word* God is dead." [16]

However, to speak at all we need to realize that behind all that we claim to know there is a "blik." This word, derived from R. M. Hare, is used to refer to a basic conviction, probably grounded in the unconscious, that cannot be falsified. The classic example is the student at Oxford who thought that all dons wanted to murder him. No evidence to the contrary could be accepted. This is, says Hare, an "insane blik," and what we need are sane ones. A blik, then, is not based on impartial evidence from without by someone who does not care, but arises from self-involvement and deep caring. It is from the focus of one's blik that he observes his world and provides his explanations. Hare writes, "Certainly it is salutary to realize that *even* our belief in so-called hard facts rests in the end on a faith, a commitment, which is not in or to facts, but in that without which there would not be any facts." [17]

The language of faith, for van Buren, even though it has no reference to God, has meaning because it is the language of

[15] Paul M. van Buren, *The Secular Meaning of the Gospel* (New York: Macmillan, 1963), p. 8.

[16] Ibid., p. 103.

[17] In Basil Mitchell, ed., *Faith and Logic* (London: George Allen & Unwin, 1957), p. 192. See Antony Flew and Alasdair MacIntyre, eds., *New Essays in Philosophical Theology* (London: SCM Press, 1955), pp. 99–103. "Blik" is a Dutch word (German *blick*) meaning "glance, look." *Si jn heldere blik* means "his keen insight." This use may or may not have a connection with Hare's.

one who has been "caught" by the gospel, whose blik is functioning, who is addressing himself to his situation in the world. This faith turns on what happened at Easter.

The idea of Jesus as "a free man" is essential to van Buren's portrayal. Jesus was free from many claims on him in terms of family, law, and authority; he was free to speak on his own authority and to do so without making any claims for himself. "He was above all free for his neighbor." [18] This, says van Buren, is the "logical meaning" of faith.

This freedom was not evident in his followers and there were "no Christians before Easter." After Easter, the disciples were changed men. "Whatever it was that lay in between, and which might account for the change, is not open to our historical investigation. The evidence is insufficient. All we can say is that something happened." "The freedom of Jesus began to be contagious." [19]

As van Buren recounts this story, he is careful about his choice and use of words. He says that "contagious" may be used in a figurative sense, as in "He has a contagious smile." "It carries the sense of our 'catching' something from another person, not by our choice, but by something which happens to us. We use it to point to the event of Easter, not of course to describe it." [20]

So we can point to the liberating effect that Jesus has on those who are gripped by him. It is the story which is central, as the Gospel narrative is essential for this work to go on. For the believer in the Easter event, the gift of freedom is offered, and the result is a meaningful life with a historical and ethical dimension. All of this can become operational without reference to assertions about God.[21]

---

[18] Van Buren, op. cit., p. 123.

[19] Ibid., pp. 128, 133.

[20] Ibid., p. 133.

[21] For evaluations of van Buren's position, see my article, "The Easter Event and Christian Education," Near East School of Theology Quarterly (April 1967); symposium, "Linguistic Philosophy and Christian Educa-

For those who rest easily and uncritically within the uses of language in the Christian community, the kinds of questions posed by the philosophers of language may lead to uneasiness and therefore rejection, or the questions may not even be considered. Yet in the world of today, we are aware that what is said is not understood, and if this is so, the blame must be placed squarely where it belongs—on those who fail to communicate.

As we turn to Christian education, we are faced first with the question of verification, which does not seem to bother such men as van Buren and Braithwaite. Then we can see how van Buren makes use of stories as stories and speaks of teaching about love. At this point we take up some hints from the distinctions between various kinds of language-games, which is a particularly important insight for Christian educators. We find that we can still talk about a world view or metaphysics, even though language is a weak stem on which to build ultimate meanings. Finally, we note some elements in the discipline of education as pointed out by Marc Belth.

Normally, when we make assertions, we do not even bring up the question of verification. Language arises from persons who speak, and the uses are as varied as the persons.[22] Language deals with experience in the broadest meaning of the word, and it is a mistake to limit its basis to a narrow interpretation of ex-

---

tion," *Religious Education*, LX (Jan.–Feb. 1965), pp. 4–42, 48; David M. McIlhiney, "Paul van Buren and the Christian Stories," *Religious Education*, LXII (Jan.–Feb. 1967), pp. 32–37; Gerard S. Sloyan, *Speaking of Religious Education* (New York: Herder & Herder, 1968), pp. 42–51; Robert L. Richard, *Secularization Theology* (New York: Herder & Herder, 1967), pp. 36–42, 49–50, 74–119; Schubert M. Ogden, *The Reality of God* (New York: Harper & Row, 1966), pp. 13–15, 85–90; E. L. Mascall, *The Secularisation of Christianity* (London: Darton, Longman & Todd, 1965), pp. 40–105.

[22] See Dallas M. High, op. cit., p. 42.

perience.[23] We know enough about the neurological system to be aware of the way in which the human brain can absorb impressions, retain concepts, understand relations, and create imaginative ideas which can be communicated to move beyond the senses as the only source or test of knowledge.

Van Buren has looked at the classroom in his article "Christian Education *Post Mortem Dei.*" [24] In this situation, "the teacher can (1) teach the Christian story, (2) clarify the relations between faith and knowledge, and (3) clarify the relations between believing and living." [25] Crucial to Christian education is the teaching of a story *as story*, leaving the telling of the story to pulpit and holy table. The stories are not to be understood as factual or critical histories, but simply as stories which can be appreciated and hopefully lead to ways of understanding and being understood.

As soon as one comes up against religious assertions, the pupils will have questions. One can verify the statement that the Rev. Mr. Blank is the rector of the parish, but one cannot in the same way verify the assertion that Jesus is Lord. Here is where clarification about language enters the educational process. Van Buren suggests that one way of resolving this issue may be found in a consideration of art. Trying to explain the beauty of a painting after it has "come alive" is different from reporting the score of a baseball game. One learns to talk about art, music, or love, but he needs to understand that the logical placing of such language is different from reporting the score of a ball game. This logical placing of the language of faith is something that must be learned.

A helpful illustration is that we cannot "teach love" but we

---

[23] See Brand Blanshard, "The Philosophy of Analysis," in H. D. Lewis, ed., *Clarity Is Not Enough* (New York: Humanities Press, 1963; London: George Allen & Unwin, 1963), pp. 80–109.

[24] *Religious Education*, LX (Jan.–Feb. 1965), pp. 4–10. Reprinted in *Theological Explorations* (New York: Macmillan, 1968), pp. 63–77.

[25] *Religious Education*, op. cit., p. 6.

can "teach about love." Van Buren suggests that the literature of love stories and poetry might be a starting point. In the process there would be a discovery of the different kinds of language that are used. But this analogy cannot be pushed too far, for "believers have stories to tell, not a photograph to look at." [26]

Wittgenstein's suggestion of the great variety of language-games is possibly the most important clue derived from this approach to language analysis. The teacher can help the student, possibly from about the age of seven, to recognize different categories of language use. For example, there is the simple distinction between factual and imaginative language. When a seven-year-old asks, "Is it true?" he has in mind empirical evidence. If he has heard Bible stories, he interprets them in a literal manner. It is at the age of from seven to eleven that we have the problem of their reducing other language-games to the descriptive, thereby providing a false base for future religious belief or for the rejection of it. Ronald Goldman's studies, supported by many others, indicate that only after the watershed of the beginning of puberty do we find the capacity to think in terms of abstract propositions and especially in terms of analogical and imageless concepts.[27]

To take another example, if a seven-to-eleven-year-old child should ask if the ascension story is true, the proper reply is "No." For in his framework, "true" means empirically and descriptively so. If the question, "How fast did Jesus go up?" is improper, we need to find a way of distinguishing between the language of myth and that of the astronauts. We can say that it is just a story, or that it is early science fiction, or that it was an

---

[26] Ibid., p. 10.

[27] See Ronald Goldman, *Religious Thinking from Childhood to Adolescence* (New York: Seabury Press, 1968; London: Routledge & Kegan Paul, 1963); Violet Madge, *Children in Search of Meaning* (London: SCM Press, 1965); Edwin Cox, *Sixth Form Religion* (London: SCM Press, 1966); Harold Loukes, *Teenage Religion* (London: SCM Press, 1963); J. W. D. Smith, *Religious Education in a Secular Setting* (London: SCM Press, 1969), pp. 71–81.

attempt of the early Christians to tell of a unique experience. The problem is one of meaning for those who told the story. We have some evidence that children of this age can deal successfully with parables and other imaginative stories in just this manner. They will say of a parable, "It's not true, but it helps me to understand."

There are a number of language-games which pupils may be helped to recognize. If I say, "Shut the window please," this is an imperative. One does not normally ask for verification of the window, but one responds by closing it. It would have nothing to do with proof if the hearer replied, "Close it yourself." Imperative language operates with meaning outside the limits of verification. "Go therefore and make disciples of all nations (Matt. 28:19)" is an imperative from a biblical source.

If John says, "I, John, take thee, Mary, to be my wedded wife," the words do something. Without these words, the marriage does not occur. The words are the act, provided that there is no impediment. The words are completed publicly, and the clergyman says, "I pronounce you man and wife." Such language is performative and self-involving, and, as we will see, is significant for Christian education. "I accept Jesus Christ as Lord and Savior" is such a performative statement.

"Art thou the man?" represents an interrogative form of speech and is equally essential for meaningful discourse. The question may be rhetorical or may be for the purpose of stimulating thought. In some cases, it demands a direct answer.[28]

Religious experience carries one into an area of mystery, and sometimes silence is the only possible result. But we try to explain and this leads to the use of paradox, sometimes in very helpful ways. John Wisdom has called paradoxes "symptoms of linguistic penetration." [29] Language is at work in such a case, even though the result does not resolve the paradox.

---

[28] See Frederick Ferré, *Language, Logic, and God* (New York: Harper & Row, 1962), pp. 55–57.

[29] *Philosophy and Psychoanalysis* (Oxford: Basil Blackwell, 1953), p. 41.

We can and do speak of a world view, of metaphysics. We need a way of looking on life and the universe as Christians. As long as a world view is rooted in empirical facts, it may provide a reasonable way of looking on things. Various maps of the world may show its mineral resources, its mountains and rivers, or its national boundaries. It may be a globe or Mercator's projection. I may need a map to get from New Haven to New York City, or a sea chart to sail to New London. In any case, I am trying to gain perspective on where I am going.[30] Ultimately, I need to connect things together, or find out that God has already done so. For the Christian, metaphysics helps place God at the center of meaning, as the key word.

The above examples may prove helpful to teachers, but what is essential is to be willing to explore these distinctions with children. The foundation of Christian education lies in the stories, myths, legends, poetry, and history of all people. Out of an attack on language and its meanings, probably in adolescence, belief in God may begin to emerge as one's own belief. In the current confusion, this is where the difficulty is greatest.

"Language," writes Brand Blanshard, "is a very dim and flickering taper with which to explore infinity, or freedom, or causality, or substance, or universals. In such questions, commonsense meanings can, at best, provide a point of departure, and one from which the critical mind makes its departure rapidly and into distant places." [31] But these distant places are difficult to talk about, and this is where the problem is most crucial. Van Buren will let us talk about Jesus and contagious freedom, but for him the word "God" does not operate. This is not a new problem, however. As far back as 1928, Henry Nelson Wieman suggested that "we do not know what we are trying to do in religious education because we have no common understanding concerning the word God. All sorts of diverse ideas are held concerning what the word stands for. . . . If we could

---

[30] See H. H. Price, in H. D. Lewis, ed., *Clarity Is Not Enough*, p. 37.
[31] In H. D. Lewis, ed., op. cit., p. 103.

banish the problem by simply banishing the word, all would be well. But it is not so simple as that." [32]

WHAT EDUCATION IS

We can be helped further with this kind of analysis if we turn our attention to some logical distinctions in the study of education. First, according to Marc Belth, we need to distinguish between education and schooling. A school is a reflection of the interests, needs, and purposes of a community and therefore does many things in the interest of the students' welfare which are not strictly education, such as concern with health, athletics, manners, citizenship, and other desirable services. A church school or a parish school may have similar concerns, plus such activities as worship, within the framework of an objective that includes indoctrination.

Education, however, says Belth, "deals with the relationship between concepts and powers nurtured in learners, and with the methods of creating concepts as the inventions of intelligence, in whatever fields these methods come to be employed. . . . Education becomes a way of raising and answering a question not otherwise asked, a question centering on the problems of improving the ability to think. . . . It is . . . concerned with the development of powers of thinking, symbol manipulation, and identification of theoretical bases for the acting and speaking, the exploring, and the describing which identify man." [33]

Education is concerned with bringing the old and the new together, so that the learner will continue to increase his powers and to find deeper meaning in the world. This goal points

---

[32] *Religious Education*, XXIII (Oct. 1928), p. 715. For some of the difficulties presented by current theologies, see Theodore McConnell, "The Scope of Recent Theology: New Foundations for Religious Education," *Religious Education*, LXIII (Sept.–Oct. 1968), pp. 339–49.

[33] Marc Belth, *Education as a Discipline* (Boston: Allyn and Bacon, 1965), pp. 7, 13, 39. See Charles F. Melchert, "The Significance of Marc Belth for Religious Education," *Religious Education*, LXIV (July–Aug. 1969), pp. 261–65.

to three criteria: (1) Expansiveness, or the pursuit of liberation, is the broadening of the base of study and the refusing to accept premature conclusions. It is the recognition that no "derived or inherited system of beliefs is beyond further inquiry." [34] (2) Exploration makes use of everything that is available in experience and moves on to a consideration of literacy as a source of further information. The power to compare, test, and evaluate must accompany any exploration. We need to remember that Germany was the most literate nation in the world when Hitler took over and used an uncritical literacy as a means for maintaining his power. (3) Analysis is the power to discover and modify structure and meaning. This needs to begin at an early age. We now have evidence, says Belth, that "children, even at the kindergarten age or earlier, learn science in a way which enables them to understand the interrelationship of elements in an operation being explored." [35] This is particularly so of mathematics. But children may also develop the power to analyze different forms of language-games and thus escape from the unwitting literalness which Goldman reports is typical in the religious thinking of those from seven to eleven.[36]

The fundamental functions of education are probably universal, although they may be stated in different forms. The suggestion of Belth is that there are supportive, preservative, and deliberative functions, which can be outlined briefly as follows:

Supportive
    1. Powers of observation or perception
    2. Sign or symbol manipulation operations
    3. Instrument skills
Preservative
    4. Memory

---

[34] Belth, op. cit., p. 41.

[35] Ibid., p. 43.

[36] See Ronald Goldman, *Readiness for Religion* (London: Routledge & Kegan Paul, 1965; New York: Seabury Press, 1968), p. 18.

Deliberative
   5. Inference making
   6. Test making and test performing [37]

Most education, especially religious education, gets cut off somewhere along the way, or there are serious omissions that make the last step impossible. The stress on the authoritative teaching of Bible or church often leads to stopping at step 4. If the learner can repeat the answer, whether a theological proposition, a catechetical response, or a Bible verse, this is sometimes satisfying. But it is not education.

It is proper, educationally, to speak of students who "do" theology or Bible study or moral analysis, utilizing the skills which we have helped them to develop. These include skills of logical analysis and straight thinking based on the gathering of sufficient data, in an atmosphere in which differing with the teacher is considered a normal response. Indeed, in one set of curriculum materials this is recognized in a teacher's guide in which there is a warning against becoming an "answer man" or calling in the clergyman as the supreme "answer man." The teacher, as an enabler or equipper or coach, no matter how expert he is as a scholar, is *in his teaching function* asked to help the student to release and develop powers of observation and reasoning that will serve him as a continuing learner.

If the above can be said of all education, what can be said that makes it "Christian" or "religious"? First, there is the subject matter to which education as a discipline is applied. Second, there are the overtones of commitment and loyalty to the object being studied, so that the personal element enters fully into the picture. Third, it takes place within a community which is empirically anchored in worship of God, who is the object of study. Fourth, the teacher, and presumably the pupil, at least potentially, are loyal members of a community of believers. There is, then, a nurturing atmosphere in which the

---

[37] See Belth, op. cit., pp. 75–76.

process of education per se is found, so that commitment is encouraged.

Belth suggests that the model of education we choose will determine both goals and outcomes. In order to help both teacher and pupil cope with the world, we need a model that is effective.[38]

One way of moving toward such a model is through a consideration of the philosophy of language. Because all education, especially in the liberal arts and in religion, is so highly verbal, we need to be able to make the distinctions between models of language use that will clarify the issues and make intelligence a competent factor in religious thinking. This is not all there is to Christian education, which is rooted in the issues which arise and the needs which exist in the lives of people, and we need to recognize this limitation in language study, but it is clear that we cannot get very far unless we know how we are using words and what our assertions mean.

First, we need to look at the kinds of intellectual operations we can use in relation to the data for thinking about God as real, and to this we turn in the next chapter.

---

[38] See Melchert, op. cit., p. 265.

III. GOD AND EXISTENCE

If God does not exist, it does little good to talk about him. "Philosophy destroys its usefulness," writes Whitehead, "when it indulges in brilliant feats of explaining away. Its ultimate appeal is to the general consciousness of what in practice we experience." [1]

There is no verification of assertions about God's existence that matches the verification of scientific assertions. This is to be expected, for language about God operates on a different level from descriptive language. "Though God has never been seen by any man, God himself dwells in us if we love one another; his love is brought to perfection within us (1 John 4:12, NEB)."

In order to approach the issue of God's existence with some degree of clarity, this chapter will examine briefly the writings of F. S. C. Northrop, Alfred North Whitehead, and Charles Hartshorne, as men who operate with similar assumptions about knowledge and metaphysics. Then we will consider some of the objections to reliance on religious experience. Against this back-

[1] Alfred North Whitehead, *Process and Reality* (Cambridge: Cambridge University Press, 1929; New York: Macmillan, 1929), p. 23.

ground, we can consider some aims of education, about which Whitehead has written. Later, in chapter 9, we will return to some of the metaphysical problems.

In the field of knowledge about God, there is no new information; yet the data we have are not convincing. Religious people have strong intuitions, deep convictions, and ultimate commitments which provide meaning and guidance for their lives, but often even they are hard pressed when they seek to support their own way of looking on God and the world. The Christian educator needs more than this, for he is asked to provide education in Christianity for others, not only to describe what it has been and is, but to use language in such a way that the learner will come to an understanding of the nature of Christianity and hopefully will discern the presence of God in his own life and commit himself to the Christian way. What we need to do is to make sense out of the evidence we have. Wittgenstein says, "The problems are solved, not by giving new information, but by arranging what we have always known." [2] If we take seriously the creativity in human nature and the language that points to and shows the rich meanings to be found in human life, we can talk about the existence of God.

CREATIVE THINKING AND GOD

F. S. C. Northrop has worked out a sophisticated approach to the knowledge of God. He is concerned with the parallels between the generalized concepts of science and metaphysics, and their relation to religious thinking. He is also concerned with depth experiences that may be called religious. He believes that *"the essence of man as a moral and spiritual being is that he is a knowing being."* [3] In man's knowledge there are important distinctions that need to be made. The first is between the given facts of nature and those artifacts made by man out of cultural,

---

[2] Ludwig Wittgenstein, *Philosophical Investigations* (2d ed.; Oxford: Basil Blackwell; New York: Macmillan, 1958), p. 47e.

[3] F. S. C. Northrop, *Man, Nature and God* (New York: Pocket Books, Inc., 1962), p. 46.

human, and bodily behavior. When these two orders are confused, as they often are, we find ourselves in a mixture of language-games and cannot extricate ourselves. The second important distinction is between concepts that result from the examination of data from experience and concepts that are postulated in the intellect. Most commonsense ideas and many scientific experiments are based on induction from the data, or at least we believe that such concepts would stand up under such testing. But there are mathematical concepts which are imageless, which are independent of experience, and which are indirectly verified by the consequences, thus providing us with knowledge of the real world.

When I go for a walk, I experience space and time, and I can arrange to meet you at a street corner. But this is different from the kind of thinking that is necessary for two space vehicles to link up behind the moon, for this latter involves the kind of imageless thinking that is essential to modern physics. Columbus did not need a sophisticated analysis to find the new world, but the astronauts did to find a way to the moon. Yet both experiences refer to the real world.

The world is known, according to Northrop, in two ways: (1) by testing data from sense experience leading inductively to propositions about reality and (2) by imageless concepts postulated by the creative imagination and tested deductively. The problem is how to bring these two realms of discourse together. They consist of two widely different families of language, and Northrop says that we need a method of correlation, or correspondence, or coordination to bring them into a single view of reality. How this "epistemic correlation" is worked out is rather technical.[4] What is essential for us is to realize that the world of Einstein with his mathematical physics and the world of Joe Doaks who knows at least that the world is not flat are the same world and that some people can move from the one to the other.

---

4 See ibid., p. 90.

This provides the beginning of a method for knowledge of God. Northrop has two crucial questions. The first arises out of his experience at a conference of philosophers of East and West, in which the concepts of "Nirvana" and "the Atman that is Brahman without differences" were considered. Nirvana is a Buddhist concept and has its meaning in an all-enveloping experience. The second phrase is used in Hinduism and has its meaning in the elimination of distinctions. Both concepts are derived from the data of mystical experience. Northrop was asked whether his phrase, "the undifferentiated aesthetic continuum," was identical in meaning. In all three cases, the phrase "without differences" is critical. It refers to one's "radically immediate experience, with all the differentiations of sensing and sensa removed, signifying nothing beyond itself." [5]

Now the question for the reader is whether the description provided by Northrop has any meaning at all. Are there moments when one is swept up into a sense of oneness, when one is overwhelmed by the vastness in which he is engulfed, when one is at one with whatever being he conceives God to be? This is a kind of mysticism, reported by many as the experience of prayer or visions and by others as drug-induced. It is the keystone of many Eastern religions, as Northrop points out, but is not as evident in a practical and activist Western culture. It is so lacking in differentiation that it exists, as William James pointed out, at the periphery of experience. This is the approach to God through experience.

Now Northrop is ready for his second crucial question. Is there a basis for believing in God as a result of the imageless thinking of mathematics and physics? If so, can this be correlated with the undifferentiated experience of the awareness of oneness? The problem is that many philosophers think of imageless thinking simply as linguistic conventions which provide guidance to control reality without referring to it. Northrop, in contradiction to such a position, claims that there is presup-

---

[5] Ibid., p. 189; also see pp. 21–25.

rience and the interpretation of experience, and when they lead to significant evidence they require a recasting of language itself. Language, as we have shown, can be very slippery, and words can only point or show but do not say.[11]

In any discussion of the language about God, an appeal to experience is primary. Whitehead writes that there is wide agreement that "religious experience does not include any direct intuition of a definite person, or individual. It is a character of permanent rightness, whose inherence in the nature of things modifies both efficient and final cause."[12] A "personal" God, whatever the word "personal" may mean, is always an inference. Yet the experience from which the inference is drawn is subject to all kinds of pressures, is open to a variety of interpretations, and in the last analysis is dominantly private and subjective.

Whitehead believes that the church has been wise in its suspicion of "a direct vision of a personal God."[13] But the intuition of the inherent rightness of things is capable of acceptance, although it is "not the discernment of a form of words, but of a type of character. . . . Mothers can ponder things in their hearts which their lips cannot express. These many things, which are thus known, constitute the ultimate religious evidence, beyond which there is no appeal."[14]

As Whitehead develops this approach, examining the views of God of Asian religions, Semitic religions, and modern pantheism, he makes a striking point: As long as God is thought of as standing outside a metaphysical world view, he is unknowable. He can only be an unproven idea. "In other words," says Whitehead, "any proof which commences with the consideration of the character of the actual world . . . may discover an

---

[11] See *Process and Reality*, p. 14.

[12] A. N. Whitehead, *Religion in the Making* (New York: Macmillan, 1926), p. 61.

[13] Ibid., p. 66.

[14] Ibid., p. 67.

immanent God, but not a God wholly transcendent." [15] This insistence on immanence is an important factor in any discussion of the knowledge of God. For once God is defined as wholly transcendent, there is no possible human knowledge of him. At the same time, Whitehead writes that God "transcends the temporal world, because he is an actual fact in the nature of things." [16]

Christianity does not start with a world view, as does Buddhism, for Christianity "has always been a religion seeking a metaphysic." [17] God, he writes, is "a non-temporal entity" and is

> exempt from inconsistency which is the note of evil. Since God is actual, he must include in himself a synthesis of the total universe. There is, therefore, in God's nature the aspect of the realm of forms as qualified by the world, and the aspect of the world as qualified by the forms. His completion, so that he is exempt from transition into something else, must mean that his nature remains self-consistent in relation to all change.[18]

Such language is highly technical, including some complex metaphysical concepts, but it indicates an approach to the meaning of God similar to that of Northrop. The emphasis on God's immanence should be noted, because most of the attempts to show that God is dead or that assertions about him cannot be verified are directed toward God as transcendent only. Perhaps here is one of the possible breakthroughs in talk about God.

Necessity and Intuition

Charles Hartshorne, who shares many of Whitehead's views, states that God is a "necessary reality." He uses the tools of language analysis to make his point. "Divinity," he writes, "is not a mere fact or fiction of the actual world, but is either nonsense, in relation to all possible states of affairs, or a necessary reality,

---

[15] Ibid., p. 71.
[16] Ibid., p. 156.
[17] Ibid., p. 50.
[18] Ibid., pp. 90, 98–99.

that is, the idea is metaphysical." [19] Such truths are "certified by meaning alone," and so we can say that "God is the *one individual conceivable a priori*." [20] Therefore, we have literal truth about God.

We may use analogy and metaphor to talk about God, "but the pure theory of divinity is literal, or it is a scandal, neither well reasoned nor honestly dispensing with reason. It is precisely the being with a necessary essence that, as such, must be definable a priori." This literal truth Hartshorne sums up as follows: "Thus God is wise—period. He is unborn—period. He is everlasting—period. He is socially aware of all beings, the actual as actual, the possible as possible—period." "Whatever is good in the creation is, in superior or eminent fashion, 'analogically not univocally,' the property of God. Thus knowledge, purpose, life, love, joy, are deficiently present in us, eminently and analogically present in God." [21]

There is a difference between what we can say literally and what we can say analogically about God. There is an abstract nature to the language used about logical inferences concerning a necessary being, but the concrete actuality, described in terms of analogy and metaphor, is something each man finally intuits for himself. However, even the literal meanings of theological terms come from men's intuitions, and we need a theological method by which we can distinguish between normal intuitions which do not lead to insights into God's nature and those more "conspicuous" but less frequent intuitions which lead to deeper understanding.

There is a parallel here to Northrop's method, for Hartshorne also builds on the combination of necessary postulates in the realm of abstraction and the intuition into the presence and nature of divine power. In developing his method, Hartshorne has provided a complex logic for analyzing such terms as

---

[19] Charles Hartshorne, *The Divine Relativity: A Social Conception of God* (New Haven, Conn.: Yale University Press, 1948), p. xiii.

[20] Ibid., p. 31.

[21] Ibid., pp. 37–38, 77.

omnipotence and omniscience so that there is a place for evil in his understanding of the nature of things, for genuine freedom, and for a deity who works through persuasion. As Whitehead says, "The power of God is the worship he inspires." [22]

Hartshorne has adapted the metaphysics of Whitehead, with the emphasis on process and on God at work in the process. He has labeled this "panentheism," a term which Schubert Ogden and John A. T. Robinson have adopted. "The concrete reality of God," says Hartshorne, "is in us only insofar as we, with radical ineffectiveness and faintness, intuit it. Though it is vastly less true to say that we do than that we do not 'have' or include God, both statements are true. God, on the other hand, in his actual or relative aspect, unqualifiedly or with full effectiveness has or contains us; while in his absolute aspect he is the least inclusive of all individuals." [23]

Northrop, Whitehead, and Hartshorne provide us with the use of technical vocabularies and dynamic metaphysical categories to talk about God. They are able to do this in a meaningful way, because they are concerned with the view of the secular world as modified by the latest scientific insights, and they speak religiously without being limited to traditional forms of language. Northrop speaks out of personal acquaintance with Wittgenstein and Whitehead as well as out of knowledge of the broad field of the philosophy of culture. Whitehead's influence is more and more permeating the current scene in philosophical theology as well as in metaphysical thinking. Hartshorne has applied a complex logic to thought about God and has influenced such theologians as Schubert Ogden, John Cobb, Kenneth Cauthen, Peter Hamilton, Norman Pittenger, and John A. T. Rob-

---

[22] A. N. Whitehead, *Science and the Modern World* (New York: Macmillan, 1927), p. 276.

[23] Hartshorne, op. cit., p. 92; see also Schubert Ogden, *The Reality of God* (New York: Harper & Row, 1966), p. 62; John A. T. Robinson, *Exploration into God* (Stanford: Stanford University Press, 1967), pp. 86, 89–96; Kenneth Cauthen, *Science, Secularization, and God* (Nashville: Abingdon Press, 1969), p. 164. See below, chapter 9, for a further treatment of metaphysics.

inson. Northrop, Whitehead, and Hartshorne, therefore, throw much light on our endeavor to speak of God in the light of current developments in linguistic philosophy and secular thinking. They at least establish the philosophical respectability of "God-talk" in the contemporary world.

SKEPTICISM AND RELIGIOUS EXPERIENCE

But we are not home free. These three men come down finally to a reliance on some form of intuition or religious experience.[24] When Rudolf Otto describes the sense of the "numinous" or holy as an irrational experience both fascinating and awe inspiring, in which the content can only be felt and not spoken about, he is making a similar point. For Otto, this "wholly other" is transcendent rather than immanent, which marks it off from Whitehead's insistence that immanence is the key, although both seem to be considering the same experiential evidence. For Otto, such experience stands alone, without value when reduced to language.[25]

A. J. Ayer is critical of propositions that result from such experiences. He writes, "In describing his vision the mystic does not give us any information about the external world; he merely gives us indirect information about the condition of his own mind."[26] One answer, provided by E. L. Mascall, is that the mystics have their own language-game, although the outsider does not have the slightest idea what it is all about.[27] Ayer would respond that even if such language is used, it would have only "emotive" meaning.

Does religious experience penetrate reality and are propositions derived from intuitions to be considered seriously? This

---

[24] See Northrop, op. cit., p. 108; Whitehead, *Religion in Making*, p. 62; Hartshorne, op. cit., p. 38.

[25] See Rudolf Otto, *The Idea of the Holy* (London: Oxford University Press, 1923; Pelican Books, 1959).

[26] A. J. Ayer, *Language, Truth, and Logic* (2d ed.; London: Gollancz, 1936), p. 118.

[27] See E. L. Mascall, *Words and Images: A Study in Theological Discourse* (London: Longmans, Green & Co., 1957), p. 12.

is a key question in any discussion of religious language. Not only must there be some agreement about the meaning of the word "God" but there must be some kind of objective reference. Ian T. Ramsey speaks of a "cosmic disclosure, an element of transcendence in both the objective reference and in our own subjective response and commitment." [28] The key to this is "the method of empirical fit." [29] You don't verify a shoe, you wear it. If it does not fit, you discard it. If, after a few wearings, it becomes fairly comfortable, even though it may not be waterproof, it does the job. So it is with theological models. Unlike models in science which may be verified, the testing is a different kind of process. Ramsey says:

> Theology is founded on occasions of insight and disclosure when . . . the universe declares itself in a particular way around some group of events which thus take on cosmic significance. These events then become, and naturally, a self-appointed model which enables us to be articulate about what has been disclosed.[30]

Many models may be used for this kind of testing. One of the weaknesses of theology has been its reliance on single model approaches. Horace Bushnell understood this clearly over a century ago. If a theologian, wrote Bushnell,

> is a mere logicker, fastening on a word as the sole expression and exact equivalent of truth, to go on spinning deductions out of the form of the word (which yet having nothing to do with the idea), then he becomes a one-word professor, quarreling, as for truth itself, with all who chance to go out of his word; and, since words are given not to imprison souls but to express them, the variations continually indulged in by others

[28] *Religious Education* LX (Jan.–Feb. 1965), p. 12.

[29] *Models and Mystery* (London: Oxford University Press, 1964), p. 17.

[30] Ibid., p. 58. See "Linguistic Models and Religious Education," *Religious Education*, LXI (July–Aug. 1966), p. 275.

are sure to render him as miserable in his anxieties, as he is meager in his contents, and busy in his quarrels.[31]

So it is that many of us have intimations of the divine. We may or may not like the words that others have used to indicate what the divine means to them. But we may be helped if we can speak of God in a framework that makes sense in today's world. This is the point at which such men as Northrop, Whitehead, and Hartshorne may be helpful to some, for not only have they laid a foundation for belief in God as real and existing, but they have done so within the framework of a modern world view.

There is no coercive and convincing evidence. There never has been and there never will be. Those who want to be absolutely sure will have to rely on their own bliks, such as Hare has described, and not on the evidence. But decisions, attitudes, and imagination have much to do with dealing with the facts and coming to conclusions, as John Wisdom has pointed out:

> Things are revealed to us not only by scientists with microscopes, but also by the poets, the prophets, and the painters. What is so isn't merely a matter of "the facts." For sometimes when there is agreement as to the facts, there is still argument as to whether the defendant did or did not exercise "reasonable care," was or was not "negligent." And though we shall need to emphasize how much "There is a God" evinces an attitude to the familiar, we shall find in the end that it also evinces some recognition of patterns in time easily missed, and that, therefore, differences as to there being any gods is in part a difference as to what is so and therefore as to the facts, though not in the simple ways which first occurred to us.[32]

[31] *God in Christ* (Hartford: Brown and Parsons, 1849), p. 50; reprinted in H. Shelton Smith, ed., *Horace Bushnell* (New York: Oxford University Press, 1965), pp. 92–93.

[32] John Wisdom, "Gods." Reprinted from *Proceedings of the Aristotelian Society*, 1944–45, in Antony Flew, ed., *Logic and Language* (Oxford: Basil Blackwell, 1951), First Series, p. 192; and in John Hick, ed., *Classical and Contemporary Readings in the Philosophy of Religion* (Englewood Cliffs, N.J.: Prentice-Hall, 1964), p. 417.

The decision one makes, therefore, is not simply of deduction or induction, or even a combination of the two, although it is more like the combination. It is, says Wisdom, like the decision of a judge in the face of a complex presentation of evidence, which involves many subtleties, including the judge's attitudes. His ruling is like an exclamation that has its own purpose and logic and value-judgment.[33] Theology is a way of calling attention to a pattern by which the facts may be seen and understood. It assists one to penetrate more deeply into the possible meanings of reality. But the reports are always incomplete, although

> by no means useless; and not the worst of them are those which speak of oneness with God. But insofar as we become one with him, he becomes one with us. John says he is in us as we love one another. This love, I suppose, is not benevolence but something that comes of the oneness with another of which Christ spoke (John 16:21). Sometimes it momentarily gains strength —Hate and the Devil do, too. And what is oneness without otherness?" [34]

Skepticism concerning the empirical base for belief in God does not seem to be supported by the evidence. On the other hand, there is no overwhelming evidence in favor of belief. It is a matter of judgment in the light of many data. We cannot spin meanings out of the words we use, but we use words to analyze, point to, and show meanings that are found in human experience at the deepest levels. The words that penetrate successfully can clarify our experiences, but not in forms of formal logic. This is, indeed, a difficult matter, partly because the most "conspicuous" intuitions are given only to the few and partly because our logic prevents us from expressing what we dimly discern. The problem of language centers in the logical mapping of religious assertions and in the further understanding of language-games.

---

[33] See Hick, op. cit., p. 420.
[34] In Hick, op. cit., p. 428.

The modern secular man, who probably cannot understand mathematical physics but has heard of the Principle of Relativity and the Quantum Theory, does not realize how much this kind of thinking penetrates his thought processes. Although he lives in a world of common sense, he knows that nuclear science, space exploration, and studies in neurology and brain chemistry are changing the picture of the world. Insofar as he thinks about God, he worries about the way in which God is related to this new view of the world. He may escape for a while into a search for the meaning of his own existence, which is essential for his well being, but if he thinks for very long, he comes back to the problem of how God is related to the world.

What Northrop has done in a necessarily limited way is to provide a beginning concept of God for the post-Sputnik world. He has mixed two areas of discourse, both of which contribute to the concept of God when interpreted in Northrop's manner. Whitehead and Hartshorne, using similar philosophical concepts, also rely on a combination of abstract thinking and particular experiences or intuitions. Religion, says Whitehead, "stands between abstract metaphysics and the particular principles applying to only some among the experiences of life." The educational problem lies in the fact that "the relevance of its concepts can only be distinctly discerned in moments of insight, and then, for many of us, only after a suggestion from without." [35]

Certain educational implications of this approach begin to become clear. First, the "conspicuous intuitions" are given only to the few. Second, "suggestions from without" are essential. Third, duty and reverence are closely related. Fourth, careful use of words must relate dogma to experience. Fifth, the solitary experience of insight must be related to the life of the community. Sixth, we must utilize these insights in accordance with our

---

[35] *Religion in the Making*, p. 31.

knowledge of child development. Finally, we turn to Northrop's illustration from baseball of God's playfulness.

If everyone does not have a "conspicuous intuition," how can we teach about them? The tendency has been to rely on the depth experience of great saints, such as Francis of Assisi, or great heroes of the Bible who had dramatic experiences, such as Isaiah or Paul. Stories of this kind have validity, but they also are clearly unreachable by most people and seem to some to have an aura of unreality, although what has been called "the mystical germ" in us may respond positively. Religion, suggests Whitehead, applies to "only some among the experiences of life," but these do not have to be peculiarly "religious." Can we not find a "religious dimension" of all experience? Or can worship still arouse the sense of the holy, so that one's emotion of awe or wonder can open one up to appropriate the experiences of others? Whitehead says:

> The essence of education is that it be religious. . . . A religious education is an education which inculcates duty and reverence. Duty arises from our potential control over the course of events. Where attainable knowledge could have changed the issue, ignorance has the guilt of vice. And the foundation of reverence is this perception, that the present holds within itself the complete sum of existence, backwards and forwards, that whole amplitude of time, which is eternity.[36]

If there is to be "suggestion from without" by means of words in order to evoke "moments of insight," we are still operating on empirical grounds, for in order for there to be a common expression of such insight there needs to be "first a stage of primary expression into some medium of sense-experience which each individual contributes at first hand." [37] Action, words, and art can then be interpreted so that a community of intuition is brought to expression in worship and response.

---

[36] *The Aims of Education* (Mentor ed.; New York: Macmillan, 1929; New York: New American Library, 1949), p. 26.

[37] *Religion in the Making*, p. 132.

This process involves a careful understanding of the use of words. For if words do not say, some point and others show. If we choose our words correctly, some will point to the area of abstraction, of principles, of patterns, of forms, of imageless concepts; others will point to the reality reached by intuition with its mystical overtones. For we are concerned that there be a moment of insight, discernment, or disclosure; that this intuition of ultimate reality be open to analysis; that upon being convinced of its truth we be free to respond in terms of our relations with men.

This is a far cry from the prosaic grammar of description of everyday events, and therefore moves beyond the meager imaginations of those who dwell only in the flat and descriptive world of sense experience. Once one is convinced that the word "God" or one of the many synonyms for the divine refers to an activity, or process, or function, or idea, or form, or being in the actual world, the language of faith becomes a possibility.

Religion, for Whitehead, begins in solitariness. However, this is only the beginning, and he has been quoted on this point many times out of context. The individual, he says, has the moment of intuition or insight for himself; he needs to see its meaning for himself, and the theological formulation of dogmas helps him to understand his insight in relation to his world view. "A dogma," writes Whitehead, "which fails to evoke any response in immediate experience stifles the religious life." The expression of belief "is the return from solitariness to society. There is no such thing as absolute solitariness. Each entity requires its environment. Thus man cannot seclude himself from society." [38] As beliefs are verified in common, there is a common language which expresses the conviction that the gospel is good news.

This approach to the understanding of religious education underscores the significance of clarity in the use of language, which is at the same time sufficiently unique to evoke new insights. Whitehead often relies on unusual or invented words in

[38] Ibid., p. 137.

order to explain his metaphysical system. The Bible, even though oriented to a different culture, provides resources for communicating its ideas because of its unusual use of poetic and mythic imagery and of the unexpected twists of logic.

It is amazing how much we know about child development, even in terms of what might be called "religious readiness," in terms of needs, aptitudes, problems, and ways of learning and thinking.[39] Yet we ignore the limitations that children have in forming concepts and in the uses of language. We do not pay attention to the greatest of all the limitations in talking about God, the Bible, or other religious issues with children, the problem of literalism. Goldman's studies show that approximately 60 percent of children below twelve years of age accept literal interpretations of biblical events. As soon as they can think in more abstract terms and make distinctions between literary forms, this percentage goes down to about 30 to 35 percent. By the time they reach fifteen years and a mental age of about seventeen and a half, only 5 percent take the stories literally, although 25 percent still show a partial literalism. This indicates why so many adolescents reject religious beliefs as they hold on to childish views too long and then cannot make the adjustment to other ways of thinking about religious stories and assertions.[40]

Children mimic adults and often acquire a considerable vocabulary of religious terms. But they are likely to put the words to use according to their experience. A child who had tea with his vicar announced, "I had tea with God." The phrase "The Lord is my shepherd" relies on some acquaintance with God, sheep, human beings, and shepherds plus the ability to

---

[39] See my *Education for Christian Living* (2d ed.; Englewood Cliffs, N.J.: Prentice-Hall, 1963), pp. 77–96 and bibliographical listing on pp. 414–17; also, Merton P. Strommen, *Profiles of Church Youth* (St. Louis: Concordia, 1963); Ronald Goldman, *Readiness for Religion* (London: Routledge & Kegan Paul, 1965; New York: Seabury Press, 1968) and *Religious Thinking from Childhood to Adolescence* (London: Routledge & Kegan Paul, 1964; New York: Seabury Press, 1968).

[40] See *Religious Thinking from Childhood to Adolescence*, pp. 75–80.

reason by analogy. Jesus as "the light of the world" is purely metaphorical in its meaning and even experiments with light will not be of much help with younger children.[41] Even children who show a natural reverence in saying prayers often get confused about the language, as in "Lead us not into Penn Station" for New Yorkers and "Lead us not into Thames Station" for Londoners. Their prayers are literal. These same children are likely to conceive of the Bible "as a book of magical veneration, written by God or one powerful holy person, . . . and is therefore to be accepted at a literal level as entirely true." [42] Only in adolescence, says Goldman, do pupils show the capacity to handle propositions, ideas, relationships in abstract terms and to treat myths, legends, and poetry properly.[43] This does not mean, however, that we need to wait for adolescence to make such distinctions. If we wait too long, the damage will have been done. If teachers are acquainted with the categories of religious language, even younger pupils can participate in the analysis and come to their own conclusions.[44] It is the only way to avoid a "two world" view, one of which will sooner or later be discarded except by those whose religious thinking is arrested at what Piaget calls the "concrete operational" level.[45]

Northrop moves cheerfully into the fantasy world in order to talk about "God's playfulness." He takes a seemingly outlandish illustration from a game of baseball, in which human beings err as they play the game within the rules:

Otherwise there would be no "booting the ball" after the manner of a clumsy and aesthetically crude, Brooklyn bum. Hear his religious language: "Blankety blank. This burns me up like hell." Nor would one in the next inning have the unsayable experience of seeing that same sinful, very human soul, the vulgar crowd still trying to boo him out of Flatbush, scoot,

[41] See Goldman, *Readiness for Religion*, pp. 32–33.

[42] Ibid., p. 81.

[43] See ibid., p. 163.

[44] See *Religious Thinking from Childhood to Adolescence*, p. 85.

[45] See ibid., p. 242.

Peeweelike, back to his right, deep into the hole between Short and Third, to come up with the ball in the smooth single motion over to First that has the Divinely Creative Omniscient Anticipation, Beauty, and Grace of a Rizzuto as he nips an Eddie Collins at First by an eyelash when the Umpire there, his ear on the ping in the baseman's mitt, his nose in the dust, and his eye on the runner's foot by the sack, snaps up his right arm, its Englishlike thumb pointing outward, with a shout that *means* "Out!" If this be not Heaven and its Judgment Day, what is? God has spoken! Yes, he has spoken, even though the fleet runner's coach does not believe God, and emphatically says so, not realizing—his acquaintance with Wittgenstein being slight—that not even the language of a Durocher can say anything.[46]

This strange poetic description helps us to point to the meaning of God's playfulness, to his lawfully regulated sportsmanship, and to his creatures who are free to err and to protest within the game. But the voice of the Lord makes the crucial decisions. Or, as Northrop concludes on this particular insight into God's nature:

> Sports do more than
> Malt and Milton can
> To point and show
> God's Ways to man.[47]

There is the additional problem of which language-game, which choice of words, which particular story will operate to assist in producing moments of insight. My guess is that chiefly among boys in baseball-conscious America or Japan, Northrop's flight of imaginative writing would be effective. I doubt that it would work with girls, or with most woman teachers, and certainly not in a culture dominated by soccer, cricket, or tennis. What this story does suggest, however, is that all religious language is logically odd, and to this issue we turn in the succeeding chapters.

---

[46] Northrop, op. cit., p. 250.
[47] Ibid., p. 251.

A Note on Expanded Empiricism

The argument in this chapter is limited to evidence which is consistent with empirically based language. One may, for example, move from a strictly empirical method to more expanded forms of empiricism. Schubert Ogden speaks of "nonsensuous perception," which involves "an awareness of our own past mental and bodily states and of the wider world beyond as they compel conformation to themselves in the present." [48] As one moves to such expanded forms of empiricism,[49] the next step is to go beyond these to the use of speculative theory, analogy, and myth in the formulation of beliefs.[50]

My own theological method has always included these enrichments of empirical procedures in a way that I hope has consistency and coherence. At any rate, it has made it possible for me to discuss the relation of theology to Christian education on a much broader basis than I am doing in this book,[51] to look carefully at the implications of biblical theology for Christian education,[52] and to deal theologically with the nature of the church.[53] In this view, a theory of revelation is essential as a basis for understanding the purpose of Christian education,[54] especially if this view of revelation is related to empiricism as in the thought of William Temple.[55]

[48] Schubert Ogden, "Present Prospects for Empirical Theology," in Bernard E. Meland, ed., *The Future of Empirical Theology* (Chicago: University of Chicago Press, 1969), p. 82.

[49] See my "Empirical Method and Its Critics," *Anglican Theological Review*, XXVII (Jan. 1945), pp. 27–34.

[50] See my *What We Can Believe* (New York: Charles Scribner's Sons, 1941), pp. 201–21.

[51] See my *The Clue to Christian Education* (New York: Charles Scribner's Sons, 1950), pp. 1–17.

[52] See my *Biblical Theology and Christian Education* (New York: Charles Scribner's Sons, 1956), pp. 16–31.

[53] See my *Christian Nurture and the Church* (New York: Charles Scribner's Sons, 1961), pp. 1–32.

[54] See "Revelation, Relevance, and Relationships," *Religion in Life*, XXVII (Winter, 1957–58), pp. 132–43.

[55] See William Temple, *Nature, Man and God* (London: Macmillan

But unless God *is*, however dim may be our awareness and however vague our formulation in language of this awareness, all the superstructures of belief lack a firm foundation. In this assertion of the existence of an actual deity, we have the basis for the doctrines of creativity and redemption. If we look on the world as created and redeemed by God, using the Bible as our guide, we have a foundation for our beliefs about God, about Christ, about the Holy Spirit, and about the church. Christology, like revelation, depends on a prior knowledge of and acquaintance with God. This is the *logical* order of the language of faith. From there we can move to broad speculations about the nature of God and the universe, using theological and philosophical tools.

The *psychological order* of coming to an attitude of faith and the development of beliefs, however, may not be and usually is not logical. One may come to share the Christian faith exclusively through belief in Jesus as the Christ, or through exposure to the life of the existing church, or through the contagion of the freedom of Christians. The moment of disclosure or discernment and the resulting commitment is not dictated by the logic of theological discourse. But if one comes to God through these other routes, as most people do, the intellectual sustaining of this faith ultimately goes back to belief in the existence of God as an "empirical anchor." Otherwise, one may be left with a Christology that is not grounded in God, as in van Buren's case, or with a church that is not grounded in worship, or with Christian behavior that is not grounded in a grace-faith relationship.[56]

One major task of Christian education, therefore, turns on the language that we can use to speak of the existence of God. This becomes the basis for all other talk about God, where there is room for speculation, imagination, fantasy, and hope.

Co., Ltd., 1934), pp. 301–27; Sara Little, *The Role of the Bible in Contemporary Christian Education* (Richmond: John Knox Press, 1961), pp. 28–33.

[56] See my *Christian Nurture and the Church*, pp. 33–35.

IV. THE PROBLEM
OF MYTH

In the first three chapters, we have considered the kinds of literary forms found in the Bible, the challenge of linguistic analysis to our teaching, and the data for any assertions about the existence of God. If "God-talk" is at least a possibility, we need to ask questions about the kinds of language that have been and can be used. One of the most perplexing of these questions has centered on the nature and use of myth.

The most popular understanding of myth is as a narrative of a purely fictitious character concerning supernatural beings. Often it is used in the sense of being a tale lacking in truth, and usually thought of as coming from some primitive or unscientific culture. Because of this, its more technical use in religious literature is frequently misunderstood. It seems like nonsense to speak of the "truth value of myth," yet the study of religious myths leads to just this assertion, for as we talk about God as in any way supernatural we move into categories of language which are other than commonsense description. Reinhold Niebuhr says:

> These mythical terms are the most adequate symbols of reality because the reality we experience constantly suggests a

center and source of reality, which not only transcends immediate experience, but also finally transcends the rational forms and categories by which we seek to apprehend and describe it.[1]

One of the major problems in communicating ideas or concepts found in the Bible derives from the use of myth as a form of language. If the pupils are led to understand that all myths are false, we have the choice either of denying that such literature is mythical or of asserting that myths carry meanings not otherwise communicable. If they are unwilling to accept the myths as they stand because of the contradictions between the biblical and modern world views, we face the difficulties of demythologizing.

BULTMANN AND MYTH

It is at this point that it is helpful to consider the contribution of Rudolf Bultmann, who has done more with New Testament mythology than most writers. Bultmann uses myth in a limited and narrow sense which cannot be identified with an ideology or with make-believe. "Mythology," says Bultmann, "is that manner of representation in which the unworldly and divine appears as worldly and human—or, in short, in which the transcendent appears as the immanent. Thus, in the mythological manner of representation, God's transcendence is thought of as spatial distance." [2] A myth puts God "out there" in space and

---

[1] Julius Seelye Bixler, Robert Lowry Calhoun, and Helmut Richard Niebuhr, eds., *The Nature of Religious Experience* (New York: Harper & Bros., 1937), p. 135; reprinted in Reinhold Niebuhr, *Faith and Politics* (New York: Braziller, 1968), p. 31.

[2] Schubert Ogden's interpretation of Bultmann is extremely helpful. He has made his own translations of the passages from Bultmann. I have followed these and have given the sources both in Bultmann's writings and in Ogden's book. For this passage, H. W. Bartsch, ed., *Kerygma und Mythos*, I (2d ed.; Hamburg: Herbert Reich-Evangelischer Verlag, 1951), p. 22, n. 2; English translation (E. T.), *Kerygma and Myth* (New York: Harper & Bros., 1961), p. 10. Schubert Ogden, *Christ Without Myth* (New York: Harper & Bros., 1961), p. 24. See Ogden's definition of myth in his *The Reality of God* (New York: Harper & Row, 1966), p. 104.

time and allows for his incursion into the sensed world of man through miracles. A myth, then, tells a story of supernatural occurrences within history and therefore results in a double view of history. For the natural man, who sees his world in terms only of secular events, such a double image is unnecessary even if possible. This is the point at which we pick up the report of Bultmann's treatment of the biblical "three-storey" universe with its unnatural causes, a world picture that is automatically rejected by modern man.

Because the modern man confuses the mythological picture of the world with the New Testament teaching about himself, sin, salvation, resurrection, and the sacraments, he rejects the total package. This leads some men to pick and choose among the myths, retaining those which are not too impossible and rejecting others, but this procedure fails to get at the root of the matter, for the radical question is whether the truth of the New Testament can exist outside its outmoded mythological picture of the world. Most men reinterpret the New Testament either unconsciously or selectively, but Bultmann claims that "if the New Testament is to maintain its validity, there is nothing else to do but demythologize it." [3]

This word "demythologizing" has been a red flag for scholars, Christian educators, and lay people. However, it is something that has been going on since the beginning of Christianity and can be found within the New Testament itself. This is especially true in the changing of expectations of the end of the age between the time that Paul wrote to the Thessalonians and the writing of the Fourth Gospel. Even the change in the choice of myths is a form of demythologizing. As one traces out the

---

[3] *Kerygma und Mythos*, I, p. 22; E. T., p. 10; Ogden, *Christ Without Myth*, p. 39. Gilbert Ryle writes, "A myth is, of course, not a fairy story. It is the presentation of facts belonging to one category in the idioms appropriate to another. To explode a myth is, accordingly, not to deny the facts but to reallocate them." What we do is to make "a category mistake." *The Concept of Mind* (London: Hutchinson & Co., 1949; Peregrine Books, 1963), p. 10.

developments of theology down to the present time, it is obvious that the process has continued.

To Bultmann, this is a cause for rejoicing, for he wants the gospel to speak to the present generation. But it is more than this, for it is "a demand of faith itself." Faith cannot be a slave to any world view, mythological or scientific. If we reflect on the self-knowledge that is essential to faith, we conclude that "it is this call that demythologization wants to follow." [4]

One way of looking at Bultmann's endeavor is to consider it as translation. It is an attempt to fit the gospel to man's condition. He has adopted the categories of existentialism, as derived from Martin Heidegger. Theological thinking, he says, is concerned with the immediate understanding of one's self as a person. This is different from thinking about one's self or one's world. It tries to get at the basic question of "Who am I?" In reading the Bible, one tries to share the experiences and the historical situation represented in the document and to look for the answer to his own question for self-understanding. The new understanding is the gift of the new creation, for God is judge now and is calling men to decide for life or death.[5] Bultmann insists on the uniqueness of each man's search for God:

> Genuine faith in God is to be sharply distinguished from what is customarily called a world-view. The knowledge of the power that creates and limits our existence is not a theoretical knowledge, but, on the contrary, is a knowledge that breaks in upon us at critical moments in existence itself. It is never possessed as a secure possession or as a quieting insight, but rather constantly has to make its way against all the temptations that continually emerge out of existence and give man the illusion he can still dispose of himself and has his life in his own hands —even if it be by virtue of just such an insight. . . . Therefore, genuine faith in God is not a general truth which I acknowledge, of which I dispose, and which I apply. On the con-

---

[4] *Kerygma und Mythos*, II, p. 207; E. T., p. 210; Ogden, *Christ Without Myth*, p. 43.

[5] See *Christ Without Myth*, p. 62.

trary, it is what it is only as something that constantly grows up and is laid hold of anew.[6]

Bultmann asserts that Jesus was a historical figure and that the crucifixion occurred as a public event. But these public facts are not the crucial ones. His main point is that the cross becomes real with personal force in one's own existence. It comes alive in *my* history (*Geschichte*) because it is already a reality in secular history (*Historie*).[7] Not all events recorded in the Bible are historical in this sense (*Historie*), as any scholar would agree, but Bultmann judges each event on its merits. What is theologically and religiously important is how it affects my history (*Geschichte*).

For Bultmann, then,

> to speak of God's act means to speak at the same time of my own existence. . . . Therefore, to speak of God's act is not to speak figuratively or symbolically but *analogically*. For in such speaking, we represent God's act as analogous to human action, and we represent the communion between God and man as analogous to the communion of men with one another. Still, the meaning of such speaking must be further clarified. Mythical thinking represents the divine action . . . as an action that breaks into and disrupts the continuum of natural, historical, or psychical events—in short, as a "miracle." . . . God's act is hidden to every eye but that of faith.[8]

---

[6] *Glauben und Verstehen* (Tübingen: J. C. B. Mohr, 1952), pp. 6 ff.; Ogden, *Christ Without Myth*, p. 67. Note how Bultmann's description is similar to Ramsey's approach described in chapter 5.

[7] "German has two words for history—*Geschichte* and *Historie*. As Bultmann uses them, the former refers to an event so far as it is significant for human existence (e.g., the cross as the salvation-occurrence through which I understand myself as judged and forgiven by God), while the latter refers to an event considered in abstraction from such significance (e.g., the cross as an incident in the annals of ancient history)." From a letter from Ogden.

[8] *Kerygma und Mythos*, II, pp. 196 ff.; Ogden, *Christ Without Myth*, pp. 91–92.

Only by demythologizing can the hidden reality of God in man's authentic existence be expressed, and of this we may speak analogically.

This brings us back to the problem of language. Bultmann suggests that there are other languages than those of science and myth. "Indeed, there is a language of faith in which existence naïvely expresses itself, and, corresponding with this language there is also a science that speaks of existence without objectifying it to worldly being." [9] Bultmann is here asking us to adopt the nonmythological language of Heidegger as having currency for today's world.

Bultmann's position is more sophisticated and complicated than this, but this is enough of a summary to indicate its possible values for Christian education. It is a position open to serious criticism, as Ogden has pointed out.[10] But it may also serve as a basis for further development of theological thinking, as we find it in Ogden's writings.

"CHRIST WITHOUT MYTH"

Ogden writes that his first principle is that "*the demand for demythologization that arises with necessity from the situation of modern man must be accepted without condition.*" [11] Ogden is willing to use mythology in both teaching and preaching, although it causes difficulty in communication unless it is understood as myth. But teaching is not complete unless myth is translated, although not necessarily into Bultmann's categories. Theology which is purely mythical and translated so that it is limited to statements about God alone is untenable. Statements about God always have implications for man, so that we can say, "theology is the truth-about-God-in-relation-to-man." [12]

---

[9] *Kerygma und Mythos*, II, p. 187; Ogden, *Christ Without Myth*, p. 56.

[10] See Ogden, ibid., pp. 99–111.

[11] Ibid., p. 127.

[12] See my *The Clue to Christian Education* (New York: Charles Scribner's Sons, 1950), p. 5.

This, however, does not make theology Christian. Here Ogden places his second principle that *"the sole norm for every legitimate theological assertion is the revealed word of God declared in Jesus Christ, expressed in Holy Scripture, and made concretely present in the proclamation of the church through its word and sacraments."* [13] The center of the gospel must be freed from myth in order to be a basis for any kind of knowledge that can be verified.

God has always made himself known, and therefore all men and men in all times are responsible and without excuse. In such a framework, we can have "Christ without myth," where he is understood as "the final reality of God's love that confronts us as sovereign gift and demand in all the events of our existence." [14]

We speak of God analogically. Whereas Bultmann uses analogy only within an existentialist framework, Ogden claims that we can think of God analogically within other philosophies. Furthermore, we can "speak of God 'analogically' without also having to speak of him 'mythologically,'" as Charles Hartshorne has made clear.[15] This can be done, says Ogden, without sacrificing Bultmann's and Heidegger's insights,[16] for there is a theocentric basis to religious belief that is beyond myth. If we think of a world view in terms of process philosophy, we can develop a way of thinking that takes account of both existential analysis and external reality.[17]

EDUCATIONAL INSIGHTS

As we turn to the educational insights to be derived from Bultmann and Ogden, we will consider the following points:

---

[13] Ogden, *Christ Without Myth*, p. 138.

[14] Ibid., p. 161.

[15] Ibid., p. 147.

[16] See *The Reality of God*, pp. 149–57, 174–87.

[17] "Unless process philosophy is informed by existential analysis, its lack of an explicit anthropology, which handicaps it for theological employment, can hardly be remedied in keeping with its own implicit principles." Ogden, *Christ Without Myth*, p. 152.

the significance of Jesus Christ, the varied uses of myth against the background of the religious issues in life, the use of objective language about God, the requirement for meaning and reassurance in teaching, the problem of being saved without knowledge of Jesus and the teaching of comparative study of religions, and the value of distinctions between myth and reality for children.

Our first point is made clearly by Ogden:

> The entire reality of Jesus of Nazareth, including not only his preaching and acts of healing, but his fellowship with sinners and his eventual death on the cross, was transparent to the word he sought to proclaim. By this is meant that the event of Jesus . . . in "its significance" confronts those who encounter it with a certain possibility of existentiell [existential] understanding.[18]

The purpose of teaching and preaching is to bring about a response, for such communication requires a decision. This is the distinction between "knowledge about" and "acquaintance with," and we are concerned primarily with the latter. The emphasis is on self-understanding and personal decision, or, in other language, on insight and commitment. This is the point at which the word existential is important in Christian education, for it confronts the hearer with such questions as "Who am I?" "Why should I?" and "Who are you?"

As Ogden indicates, this can be expressed in nonmythological language: "Jesus' office as the Christ consists precisely in his being the bearer, through word and deed and tragic destiny, of the eternal word of God's love, which is the transcendent meaning of all created things and the final event before which man must decide his existence." [19]

A second educational insight surrounds the specialized use of the word myth. It is "the report of an occurrence or an

---

[18] Ibid., p. 159.
[19] Ibid., p. 160; see also Rudolf Bultmann, *Jesus and the Word* (2d ed.; New York: Charles Scribner's Sons, 1958), pp. 212–19.

event," says Bultmann, "in which supernatural or superhuman powers or persons are at work. . . . Myth objectifies the transcendent and thus makes it immanent." [20] The problem is that of language-games, in which mythological language is contradicted by scientific language about the same world. If God is conceived as a subject addressing man in his self-awareness, neither language is suitable, for language about the external world is inadequate for expressing existential self-awareness. It has become an impossible situation, because man can no longer think about the world in mythological terms and must think existentially about the meaning of his life. Therefore, in order for the Christian myths to be communicable and understandable, they must be demythologized into existentialist language. This is the primary distinction that must be accepted in order to use Bultmann's insights in Christian education.

Another way of resolving the problem is that of Amos Wilder, who understands the language of mythology to be similar to that of poetry. If this is so, then the imagery of myth *recognized as myth* may be used as a means of self-understanding and of interpreting this world as God's world. Ogden agrees that myth may be used educationally in this way.

The danger is that myths when improperly presented may degenerate into unbelievable fairy stories. A boy came home from his first day at Sunday school and his father asked him what he had learned. He replied with a story about Moses, who placed his people on trucks, drove to the edge of the water where his soldiers built a pontoon bridge, and just after the Jews crossed the bridge the enemy appeared, so the engineers blew up the bridge and all Pharaoh's soldiers were drowned. The father objected to such a tall tale, and the boy replied: "But Dad! If I told you what the teacher really said, you would never believe it!" [21]

On the other hand, when we approach such stories in terms

---

[20] *Kerygma und Mythos*, II, pp. 180, 184; Ogden, *Christ Without Myth*, pp. 24–25.
[21] See *Religious Education*, LX (Sept.–Oct. 1965), pp. 368–69.

of complete demythologizing, we are left with existential categories only. If we were consistent at this point, we could probably omit most biblical myths and recommend that the students relate to each other the stories of their own lives in terms of the achievement of self-understanding and "authentic existence." I can see how this approach might be helpful, but there would remain the question of a reference point in the Christian tradition to assist the students in their specifically Christian outlook and commitment.

If we start our teaching with the religious issues in the lives of students, as David Hunter suggests,[22] we still have to deal with the relationship of these issues to the work of God and the church, to the biblical stories, and to the consequences for Christian living. This may be done by placing existential analysis within the framework of a metaphysics in which God works nonmythologically, by interpreting God as working in public history (*Historie*) as well as in personal history (*Geschichte*), and by seeing myth as the opportunity for externalizing the issues from which the students started.[23] Such an approach makes it possible to look on the world in such a way that one finds meaning in these issues of daily life and sees them as religious.

The concept of myth, then, helps us in at least three ways. (1) If we take seriously the "truth value" in myth, as Reinhold Niebuhr suggests, we are enabled to look for the same kind of meaning in a myth that we find in a parable. (2) Because we believe we can find truth through myth, we are not threatened when we discover in the light of our twentieth-century mentality that we must reinterpret many biblical incidents as myths. These two distinctions are equally important, for the first assists us in gaining a more adequate biblical basis for interpreting the meaning of our lives and the second helps us to maintain our intellectual integrity in the face of our knowledge in other

---

[22] See David R. Hunter, *Christian Education as Engagement* (New York: Seabury Press, 1963), pp. 32–48.

[23] See Jerome Bruner, *On Knowing* (Cambridge, Mass.: Harvard University Press, 1962), p. 32.

fields. But this leads to a third problem which arises from the second. (3) If many stories may be interpreted as myth, how are we to protect the historical basis of Christian belief? It seems to me that we have enough integrity in our historical scholarship, even if we rely on the secular canons of historicity, to be clear that much of what the Bible records is history or is based on reminiscence of actual events. Within the Christian way of looking on history, these secular events may also be interpreted as evidence of God's activity in history and as revelation. This latter point matters greatly, for it is far too easy to say with the skeptics that even if the entire historical base of Christianity were swept away, Christianity would still be "existentially true" (whatever that means). The Christian claim, however, is based on historical events and human experience, as I see *my biblical onlook* operating.

A third educational insight comes from Ogden's thought as he moves beyond Bultmann into a concern for objective language. Ogden is able to speak of "the truth-about-God-in-relation-to-man" within the framework of a view of reality in which God exists. Language about God in existential terms is grounded in objective reality because God is a creative agent in the world beyond man. Also, there is a Christ event in history with evidence available in terms of secular data, although the existential element helps to make clear its significance in terms of decision. Thus objective language is as necessary as existentialist language in talk about God.

A fourth implication for our interpretation of Ogden's thought is the existential demand for meaning or reassurance. At this point, Ogden makes use of the thought of one of the language philosophers, Stephen Toulmin.[24] It is "the function of religious assertions to provide 'reassurance,'" says Ogden. "Logically prior to every particular religious assertion is an original confidence in the meaning and worth of life, through which not simply all our religious answers, but even our religious

24 See Stephen Toulmin, *The Place of Reason in Ethics* (Cambridge: Cambridge University Press, 1950), pp. 202–21.

questions first become possible or have any sense." [25] Such confidence or reassurance is directly relevant to our living in a world which provides both scientific explanations and moral responsibilities. One may act scientifically or morally without considering religious questions, but if we follow our scientific or moral reasoning to the final limits, we are faced with religious questions. Furthermore, no religious thinking is completed until it involves the whole of life.

From the point of view of Christian education, the logically prior original confidence cannot be completely lacking psychologically if we hope to assist in the building of faith. As this confidence is reassured in the nurturing process and by means of the living symbols of worship and life in community, faith is strengthened. As Ogden puts it, "religious assertions can serve to reassure us only because they themselves are the re-presentation of a confidence somehow already present prior to their being made." [26] When that confidence is absent, many religious assertions seem to be like shouting in the dark that the light is shining. Even the language of faith needs something to build on, for confidence is more than words and must arise from the relationships of home, church, school, and community.

One final question is faced by Ogden, and it needs to be answered on two levels. It is the question so often asked in high school classes, either in relation to the study of other religions or of missions: Can people be saved without Jesus? According to Ogden, they can. He cites the Bible as a basis for this belief.[27] Men have found God otherwise than through faith in or knowledge of Jesus of Nazareth. There is a subtle point to be made here, and Ogden refers to Frederick D. Maurice, who wrote:

> If we do and must attach virtues to heathens, then we do and must suppose that their virtues had their source "in the grace of Christ and the inspiration of his Spirit." Those who regard

---

[25] *The Reality of God*, pp. 32, 34.

[26] Ibid., p. 34.

[27] Romans 1:18 ff.; 3:21; 4:3, 16. See *Christ Without Myth*, p. 154.

Christ as merely a man born at a certain time into this world, and the head of a sect called Christians, may stumble at such an assertion.[28]

If Christ is eternal, if he was offered to mankind before and after he came in the flesh, which Maurice claims is orthodox belief, then we can say that Christ spoke through the prophets and speaks today. In any literal sense, this may be interpreted as being independent of Jesus. So we can say that Christ or the Word or the Logos or the Second Person of the Trinity has always been universal and has manifested himself in many ways to all people. But Ogden, while agreeing with this approach, also claims that Jesus is the "decisive manifestation" and is of unique significance. This point of view is not an argument against missions but for respect for others' faiths. It also provides a background for prior belief in God's existence and activity as a basis for understanding the significance of Jesus as the Christ for Christian faith.

Respect for those who know God without reference to Jesus of Nazareth, however, does not provide the Christian basis for faith. For theology to be Christian, the norm is Jesus Christ as found in scripture, proclamation, sacraments, and teaching. The "event Jesus of Nazareth" is "the decisive manifestation of this divine love," [29] for God works through the cross and "the entire reality of Jesus of Nazareth" provides the possibility of existential understanding. There is a sense in which the Jesus of history (*Historie*) becomes the Jesus of *my* history (*Geschichte*) which is possible when the "theocentric basis and sanction" [30] for belief in Jesus as the Christ is recognized.

> Thus to affirm that Jesus is Lord is to affirm that the final promise in which we place our confidence is none of the many promises of the so-called gods of heaven and earth, but solely

---

[28] *Christ Without Myth*, p. 155, as quoted by Alec Vidler, *The Theology of F. D. Maurice* (London: SCM Press, 1948), pp. 79 ff.

[29] *Christ Without Myth*, p. 153.

[30] Ibid., p. 143.

the promise of God's unending love to all who will but receive it. Likewise to affirm that Jesus Christ is Lord is to affirm that no demand may ultimately claim us except the one demand that we accept God's love for us and thereby be freed to fulfill his command to love all others whom he already loves. *To affirm this promise and this demand is the real meaning of affirming the lordship of Jesus Christ.*[31]

So when the high school student asks if Muslims or Buddhists can be saved, he is facing the question of whether he as a Christian can be saved. When he shows an interest in world religions, he is not (as is often thought) evading the problem of understanding Christianity, but he is asking a question that makes possible existential understanding as a Christian. If we miss this point, we fail to see the significance of our teaching about Jesus Christ.[32] Incidentally, however, by comparing what he knows about Christianity with what he can learn about other religions, he can achieve a perspective by which to understand the uniqueness of the Christian tradition and to face up to the meaning of the Christian mission. Even the comparison of the mythologies of the various religions will help him to understand more clearly the significance of the myths of the Christian tradition.

Bultmann, then, must be taken seriously by all religious teachers, for even young children need to identify the kinds of language-games they are playing. Before the age of five, they are content with almost any story, and the problem is to find ones that relate to the issues they are facing. But soon after the age of six, they can identify myths and want to know which stories are "true" (meaning factual). If we let them explore possible meanings in "just a story," they can begin to seek their own meaning and do some elementary demythologizing.

If primary school children are facing sibling rivalry in the

---

[31] *The Reality of God*, pp. 203–4.

[32] For an example of this kind of approach at its best, see Ninian Smart, *World Religions: A Dialogue* (London: SCM Press, 1960; Penguin Paperback, 1966), a text for advanced high school or college students.

family, they may be helped with the story of Cain and Abel to understand themselves. They can handle this story as a myth without trying to demythologize it, but as they identify with "Am I my brother's keeper?" (or baby-sitter?), it will take on existential significance.

The value of demythologizing for children from seven to twelve is that it guards against their tendency to take such stories literally. If Goldman is right, the literal option at this age level almost guarantees rejection of both story and meaning when the student moves into puberty (unless his mental development is arrested at what Piaget calls the concrete operational level). But at this age, as at later ages, they are also going to ask, "What really did happen?" At this point, we need to make distinctions between language that can be supported by historical data and language which operates on other levels. Ogden provides some distinctions that may help us find the criteria for such teaching. If religious faith is to provide reassurance, we need to be able to say that "God is" or "God exists" and that "Jesus lived, said and did certain things, and died" and that "the disciples experienced new life which they identified as the risen Lord." Often, however, our language refers to these experiences in categories other than the descriptive and historical and in assertions which are logically odd. Therefore, we need to explore other possibilities of linguistic expression.

V. DISCERNMENT
AND COMMITMENT

So far we have been looking at religious language in terms of natural theology and natural religion. We have been concerned to show that there is a God about whom we may speak. We have not dealt with a supernatural revealed theology, except to suggest that when men think of God as "wholly other" it is difficult if not impossible to talk of God so that men will understand.

We now turn to a position which has become for me a watershed in thinking about religious language. It is the point at which the "light dawned" in my own consideration of the use of words in Christian education.[1] The key book is *Religious Language*, by Ian T. Ramsey, now Lord Bishop of Durham.[2] "The central problem of theology," he writes, "is how to use, how to qualify observational language so as to be suitable currency for what in part exceeds it—the situations in which theology is founded."[3]

[1] See my *Christian Nurture and the Church* (New York: Charles Scribner's Sons, 1961), pp. 88–94.

[2] *Religious Language* (London: SCM Press, 1957; New York: Macmillan Paperback, 1963).

[3] Ibid., p. 38.

This involves some kind of empirical grounding for religious assertions if the language of faith is to be meaningful. Ramsey makes three important points:

(i) The need to peg back all our assertions into an awareness of God.

(ii) The need to be circumspect of any too extensive systematization, of any cut-and-dried theology.

(iii) The recognition that lack of such logical circumspection can lead to blunders which darken the light of God.[4]

"Being sure in religion," he writes, "does not entail being certain in theology." [5] Theology can be tested by its stability in the face of many data and its ability to incorporate them into a meaningful whole. This is similar to the work of an archeologist who applies his theory to a gathering of stones and who discovers that one conceptual theory may fit better than another, but this is not real deduction. Furthermore, "it is a built-in hazard of disclosures, as contrasted with 'facts' provided by scientific reporting, that they give rise to no self-guaranteed assertions." [6]

This thesis, we will see, comes up in a variety of ways in Ramsey's thought. It is derived from Joseph Butler's statement that "probability is the very guide of life." By this, he does not mean that we have nothing but doubt and uncertainty, but he does mean that in practical matters a man must act against the odds, and does it reasonably when he does so. It is similar to the position of William James, who saw clearly that there were living, forced, and momentous options facing men and that to sit on a fence waiting for evidence that is not available is to make a negative choice. Loyalty and commitment operate in areas in which theoretically we have only probability. We act in important situations when the odds are only even and sometimes

4 On Being Sure in Religion (London: Athlone Press, 1963), p. 16.
5 Ibid., p. 47. See Ramsey, Christian Discourse (London: Oxford University Press, 1965), p. 89.
6 Christian Discourse, p. 25.

when they are against us, as when a child is drowning and one tries to save him in spite of being a poor swimmer.[7]

RELIGIOUS SITUATIONS

The power of Ramsey's discourse arises as much from his illustrations as from his analyses of religious language, which makes it difficult to summarize his position without repeating his examples. He describes religion primarily in terms of "discernment" or "disclosure" and "commitment."

In religious language, he says, "we use phrases that are in certain ways odd, peculiar, and unusual." When these phrases are sufficiently parallel to discernment, "they 'come alive' . . . ; the 'light dawns' . . . ; the 'ice breaks' . . . ; the 'penny drops,' " and a disclosure is evoked in the other.[8]

In such characteristically personal situations, new insights may come over one in various ways. The use of a nickname, the humorous situation that "breaks the ice" at a stuffy party, swearing which offends the pious because it is close to the logic of the language about God, the use of words with a specialized meaning and enclosed in quotation marks or inverted commas, the discovery of someone's name after an encounter on an impersonal level are incidents which may lead to discernment. Such situations, common in everyday life as well as in religious situations, have, says Ramsey "an *objective* reference and are, as all situations, *subject-object* in structure." [9] They achieve "depth" alongside subjective changes.

A response of commitment accompanies a discernment in "a characteristically religious situation." When one faces a situation, however simple or complex, his response is in terms of freedom, which may or may not be based on a sense of duty or loyalty. Even the commitments may operate on different levels.

[7] *Religious Language*, pp. 15–17; *Christian Discourse*, pp. 23–24. See William James, *The Will to Believe and Other Essays* (New York: Longmans Green & Co., 1897), pp. 2–11, 96–103.

[8] *Religious Language*, p. 19.

[9] Ibid., p. 28.

One may make a partial commitment to mathematical axioms, recognizing that there are options although the axioms are universal in their range. One may make a complete commitment to cricket or baseball, so that it infiltrates one's whole life, but obviously it is not universal in its claim. "Religious commitment," suggests Ramsey, "combines the total commitment to a pastime, to a ship, to a person, with the breadth of mathematical commitment." [10] It is something that "grips" us; it takes a personal revolution to accept it, and once accepted it takes another conversion to reject it.

The Christian "cosmic commitment on Christ" is expressed in ordinary language used in logically odd ways. Ramsey calls this "object language and more," that is, language which "exhibits logical impropriety." One notes that religious language is like that expressed in personal situations, suggesting that "I-talk" and "God-talk" are logically related. Ramsey suggests that the logic of nicknames is akin to the use of such a term as "Son of man" by Jesus.[11] Ordinary words are strained or are mixed with others in unusual ways.

The key words of religion, says Ramsey, are found in "significant tautologies." When we force someone to a final explanation of why he did something, he will say, "Because I chose to do it," or one step further, "Because I am I." We also talk about "Duty for duty's sake" or say that "God's will is my conscience." We also say, "God is love." This, says Ramsey, is not a platitude but "a significant tautology labelling a commitment." [12]

Ramsey's conclusion is "that for the religious man 'God' is a key word, an irreducible posit, an ultimate of explanation expressive of the kind of *commitment* he professes. It is to be talked about in terms of the object-language over which it presides, but only when this object-language is qualified; in which case this qualified object-language becomes also currency for

---

10 Ibid., p. 35.
11 See ibid., pp. 137–43.
12 Ibid., p. 46.

that odd *discernment* with which religious *commitment,* when it is not bigotry or fanaticism, will necessarily be associated.

"Meanwhile, as a corollary," continues Ramsey, "we can note that to understand religious language or theology we must first evoke the odd kind of situation to which I have given various parallels." [13] This provides a basis not only for theology and communication, but for an understanding of Christian education.

MODELS AND QUALIFIERS

The word model is just beginning to have widespread use in theology, but it has been a staple of scientific thinking for many years. The most elementary model is a scale or picture model, from which someone may make something. The mock-up of a new automobile shows what it will look like when manufactured. Models of airplanes are tested in wind tunnels. Theology has used picture models for God as king or judge operating in a heavenly kingdom.

Models assist one to be articulate, to make accurate descriptions, or to take a familiar situation in order to reach a less familiar one. Scale or picture models rely on identity. But some models reproduce the structure and only approach what is to be reproduced. Max Black calls these latter, "analogue" models. Ramsey further modifies Black's view with what he calls "disclosure" models, for these rely on the "similarity-with-a-difference" that produces insight.[14] Science also uses such models to generate insight, especially when direct empirical verification is impossible, although they may be indirectly verified in crucial experiments. So also, theological models may make discourse possible, simplify complexities, and point to what otherwise eludes us. They are tested by what Ramsey calls "empirical fit" or "empirical accord" rather than by means of data specified by verifiable deduction.

Ramsey cautions us never to be satisfied with any one

[13] Ibid., p. 47.
[14] Ibid., pp. 47 ff.

model. Any model will prove too limiting, one-sided, or if pressed too far actually false. The most reliable religious discourse has the widest possible range of models. Of course, some models are more fertile than others. They need to be "suitably contextualized in a multi-model discourse." [15] Furthermore, Ramsey warns that our discourse must fit the world around us, for otherwise we will be talking nonsense. Just as in a previous time talk about seed time and harvest was suitable, so today we need to find relevance for our models in dark streets and traffic jams. A suitable model refers to God, on the one hand, and illuminates the situation, on the other; we must be careful about both reference and preference.

Ramsey's interpretation of models is helped by comparing them with similes and metaphors. A simile is like a pictorial model, as when we say that a seasick person is "as green as a leaf." A metaphor is more like a disclosure model. It opens up many possibilities of articulation, but chiefly it is a means of disclosure. "Metaphors, like models," says Ramsey, "are rooted in disclosures and born in insight." [16] They disclose but do not explain a mystery. Two realms of thought meet in a tangential manner, which at first sight may seem eccentric, and each language illuminates the other, although in "the most selective and subtle way." [17] What is disclosed includes them both but is no mere combination.

Ramsey points out that his position is similar to that of Max Black, even to agreement that both science and the humanities build on imaginative insights. But Ramsey emphasizes the word disclosure to point to the objective reference. The objective reference in theology, however, is mystery, and therefore there is always a logical gap between the model used and the disclosure that occurs. Theology thrives on a diversity of

---

[15] Ramsey, "Talking About God: Models Ancient and Modern," F. W. Dillistone, ed., *Myth and Symbol* (London: SPCK, 1966), p. 85.
[16] *Models and Mystery* (London: Oxford University Press, 1964), p. 50.
[17] Ibid., p. 52.

models which leads to "life by a thousand enrichments" rather than the death of God "by a thousand qualifications." [18]

Because all models are inadequate and diversity is essential for religious discourse, every model needs "qualifiers." These qualifiers are not further descriptions, for their logical status is not that of labels: rather they point the model in such a way that disclosure becomes possible.[19] Models do not provide blueprints or descriptions of God, but when properly qualified they do present such improprieties as may lead to discernment.[20]

When we speak of God as "first cause," "first" is a qualifier. This is a way of placing God as prior to all causes, and various stories can be told or analyses pressed back until the "light dawns." "First" does not have the logical position of "proximate" or "remote," which are adjectives. The similar grammatical structure does not imply a similar logical structure. Ramsey uses "infinitely wise," "infinitely good," and "eternal purpose" for a similar kind of logical analysis. In each case the qualifier makes the difference, changing the logical function of the key word as applied to God. This is particularly clear in his treatment of "creation *ex nihilo*." We use the word creation to apply to everything from the making of a Dior dress to painting an abstract picture to the birth of a dog. But when "*ex nihilo*" qualifies the model "creation," one does not take this literally as "making something out of nothing" but as the expression of "a sense of one-sided dependence." Furthermore, it "places 'God' as a 'key' word, for the universe of 'creatures.' " [21] When a disclosure occurs, it becomes a present claim about God and not a discussion of Genesis as a past story.

In these illustrations, Ramsey speaks of "positing the word 'God,' " but notice that he never speaks of "positing God."

---

[18] Ibid., p. 60; also see Max Black, *Models and Metaphors: Studies in Language and Philosophy* (Ithaca, New York: Cornell University Press, 1962), p. 221.

[19] Ibid., p. 60; *Religious Language*, p. 62.

[20] See *Religious Language*, p. 164.

[21] Ibid., p. 73.

"Theology is after all only *our* way of *talking* about God." [22] Ramsey says that "God-talk" is both meaningful and objective in reference. But we do not invent a particular model with its proper qualifier to "produce God. That would be semantic magic." [23] We cannot guarantee a disclosure.

LANGUAGE OF THE BIBLE

Did the writers of the Bible use such logically odd language? They certainly did, but Ramsey realizes, of course, that they did not do so explicitly. Only recently have we had the need for this kind of logical examination. One of the reasons that we cannot write a history of Jesus is that the Gospels do not pay much attention to historical method as we know it today. The Fourth Gospel's key is: "The Word became flesh." "Flesh" is a descriptive physical word, but "the Word" (*logos*) refers to a realm of discourse that is primarily abstract. Yet "Word" and "flesh" are joined by "became," a "link word," says Ramsey, that cannot be modeled. "To understand it there has to be evoked just the kind of situation which 'The Word became flesh' expresses." [24]

If we use the logically odd phrase "Word of God" to describe the Bible, with "Word" as the model and "of God" as the qualifier, so that we speak of "hearing" God's Word, we mean that if we follow the verbal pattern formed by the words of scripture, we may find ourselves in a situation in which a disclosure occurs; the "light dawns" or the "ice breaks." We do not dare to treat the Bible as straightforward logic or history, even though it contains such, if we want to discern the objective reality and mystery to which it points.[25]

The logical oddness of biblical language, with its riotous mixture of phrases, is perhaps best illustrated in Peter's sermon in Acts: "This Jesus, God raised up, and of that we are wit-

---

22 Ibid., p. 74.
23 Ibid., p. 99.
24 Ibid., p. 103; also see *Christian Discourse*, pp. 1–27.
25 See ibid., pp. 106–7.

nesses. Being therefore at the right hand of God, and having received from the Father the promise of the Holy Spirit, he has poured out this which you see and hear. . . . Let all the house of Israel therefore know assuredly that God has made him both Lord and Christ, this Jesus whom you crucified (Acts 2:32–33, 36)." These words, put together in a riotous mixture that was foolishness to the Greeks and a stumbling block to the Jews, evoked a disclosure. Look at the strange qualifiers: the *raised* Jesus, a *crucified and risen* Messiah, God has made him *Lord and Christ*, whom *you* crucified. Jesus is the key word, and the odd qualifiers that do not fit normal expectations made possible discernment and commitment. They were not convinced by argument but were "cut to the heart." We may believe that Peter's sermon on Pentecost was successful, for it is recorded that three thousand were baptized. His sermon was the *kerygma* in rough and ready form, before it had even been demythologized in later New Testament documents—much less by Bultmann.[26]

"God" is a key word for religious assertions. We may speak of God as mystery, using many models and qualifiers in order to express our beliefs. Men "posit talk of God" in a variety of ways, but this does not necessarily mean that God as objective reality lacks unity or identity. When we say that "God has disclosed himself" or "revealed himself," we are not moving into a new realm of human knowledge. Ramsey's use of discernment is similar to William Temple's interpretation of revelation. Temple writes that unless one sees revelation in the rising of the sun, one is not likely to see it in the rising of the Son of Man from the dead. Revelation is "the coincidence of a particularly revealing event and a particularly appreciative mind." [27] The point is that this is the way knowledge occurs in both the secular and the religious fields of knowledge, and any concepts resulting from the insights of the "mind divinely illumined" must

---

[26] See ibid., pp. 154–56.

[27] William Temple, *Nature, Man and God* (London: Macmillan & Co., Ltd., 1934), p. 306.

be fully tested for consistency, coherence, and "empirical fit." [28] There is a logical "impropriety" that is not the same as "irrational" or "nonrational" in that the oddity of the logic of religious language makes possible the evocation and articulation of key insights. There are grounds in such a claim for a distinction between dreams or hallucinations and religious assertions that point to and express the nonobservable.

The word God also functions as the "integrator word" in metaphysics, just as the word I functions as an "integrator word" in individual experience. Just as the word I is elusive, even when used by myself, and seemingly transcends the experience that others have of me, so also "God" is a word that eludes any set empirical formulas. Thus Ramsey writes that " 'God is active' links any and all descriptive assertions about the Universe, such as science in particular specializes in." [29] This is why the word transcendent appears in Ramsey's writings; but it is not always clear whether he is stressing the "transempirical" as a concept of imageless thinking or whether there is a "nonobservable" beyond all human endeavor; if it is the latter, there is a question whether we have any right to be articulate about it.

One other element in Ramsey's thought has been developing; this is the need for models that arise out of situations of interpersonal relationships. The concept of substance is outmoded in reference to both the human person and to God. Recent studies in both the interpersonal and existential nature of man provide new models for biblical and theological concepts. Not only do interpersonal relationships offer possibilities for dis-

---

[28] See W. D. Hudson, "Discernment Situations: Some Philosophical Difficulties," *Scottish Journal of Theology*, XIX (Dec. 1966), pp. 435–45, for some criticisms of these knowledge claims.

[29] Ian T. Ramsey, ed., *Prospect for Metaphysics* (New York: Philosophical Library, 1961; London: George Allen & Unwin, 1961), p. 174. See William H. Poteat, "God and the 'Private-I,' " Dallas M. High, ed., *New Essays on Religious Language* (New York: Oxford University Press, 1969), pp. 127–37.

closure situations, but it is likely that "a theology of relationships" may provide a superstructure for the foundation of belief in the reality of God. Once belief in God is supported in terms of "empirical fit," it is legitimate to expand concepts relating to God in terms of models derived from interpersonal relations. This approach may lead to new models and qualifiers for assertions about God, partly along the lines of thought of Martin Buber, John Oman, and H. H. Farmer.[30] In Christian education, Reuel L. Howe has made use of such models.[31]

IMPLICATIONS FOR CHRISTIAN EDUCATION

Ramsey's contributions to Christian education theory are both direct and indirect. He defines the purpose of Christian education, makes clear the place of theology, suggests that a variety of words and models be used, provides a basis for the selection of stories and parables, and seeks to anchor the process in worship. He then makes specific suggestions about the use of the past, dialogue with other disciplines, illumination of strange logical forms, the need for new models, and finding those situations to which religious language can speak.

The purpose of Christian education, in Ramsey's view, should be quite clear. It is

> to teach insight, to evoke disclosures in which we come to ourselves when and as we discern a word which has "come alive" in some particular situation. . . . What Christian education in particular seeks to do is to create this response and this fulness of life—this commitment—in relation to a discernment

---

[30] See Ramsey, "Contemporary Philosophy and the Christian Faith," in *Religious Studies*, I (Oct. 1965), pp. 53, 57–58. See also Martin Buber, *I and Thou* (2d ed.; New York: Charles Scribner's Sons, 1958); John Oman, *Grace and Personality* (Cambridge: Cambridge University Press, 1917; New York: Association Press, 1961); H. H. Farmer, *Towards Belief in God* (New York: Macmillan, 1943) and *God and Men* (Nashville: Abingdon Press, 1961).

[31] See Howe, *Man's Need and God's Action* (New York: Seabury Press, 1953).

which occurs around the person of Jesus Christ as discovered in the Bible, in doctrine, and in worship.[32]

Within this framework are places for stories, parables, poetry, and other proper logical placings of religious language in terms of models and their qualifiers, metaphors, and analogies. The empirical base is grounded in worship and interpersonal relations. Theological analysis is proper within this framework of the appropriate logical mapping of phrases. History is taken seriously, but the existential note is at the center, for discernment followed by commitment involves self-understanding and self-involvement as well as relation to objective reality.

Dogmatism has no place in this system. Ramsey writes:

> Let us always be cautious of talking about God in straightforward language. Let us never talk as if we had privileged access to the diaries of God's private life, or expert insight into his descriptive psychology so that we may say quite cheerfully why God did what, when, and where.[33]

He speaks of being "sure in religion, while being tentative, but contextually tentative in theology." [34] We start from an original context but we operate in our own context. Although our beliefs are grounded in a disclosure from God, we never reach a complete understanding of the divine mystery.

Theology, Ramsey reminds us, is built out of ordinary language used in a logically odd way. As we will see in the next chapter, this is similar to Horace Bushnell's theory of the origin of theological words, but points to the unexpectedness of the way in which words are related. Also, Bushnell and Ramsey are agreed that a great variety of words must be used, for the goal is to keep on with words and phrases, models and qualifiers, until, hopefully, a disclosure occurs. In principle, any story

---

[32] Ramsey, "Christian Education in the Light of Contemporary Empiricism," *Religious Education*, LVII (Mar.–Apr. 1962), p. 95.

[33] *Religious Language*, p. 91.

[34] *On Being Sure in Religion*, p. 90.

may lead to the desired discernment,[35] as is clear from our previous consideration of the positions of Braithwaite and van Buren. But Ramsey backs off from this conclusion, for it could lead to a "fantasy world." History, theology, and logical criteria such as coherence govern the choice of stories.

Says Ramsey:

> Christian stories must be so told in Christian education that while as a *sine qua non* they lead to disclosures, and while even a secular world may value them for the commitment they create, they also arise out of historical events that not only safeguard the relevance of theology in terms of which the disclosures are explicated, but ensure also a reference to that element of transcendence without which the good news might be less than it might be.[36]

The choice of stories is governed by the comparison of the context of the original story with the current context, taking into consideration what it might mean at various levels of development. The choice may be a biblical story, but there are many stories from all kinds of sources that may serve the purposes of Christian teaching. It is a warning to all teachers that motion pictures using biblical themes often have less religious significance than secular ones that deal with the real issues of life. Biblical stories when properly related to life have power, but if they are wrongly mapped in a prosaic or literal framework they sink to the level of a Cecil De Mille spectacular motion picture.

Parables, which are not stories about historical characters or about empirically descriptive events, have similar power, and for a very good reason. Ian M. Crombie says:

> The point of a parable is that you do not suppose that there is any literal resemblance between the truth which is expressed and the story which expresses it, but you do suppose that if you

---

[35] See *Religious Language*, p. 80.

[36] "Discernment, Commitment and Cosmic Disclosure," *Religious Education*, LX (Jan.–Feb. 1965), p. 13.

accept the story, not as a true literal account, but as a faithful parable, you will not be misled as to the nature of the underlying reality.[37]

Here is a principle which may be applied to many teaching devices. If the teacher prefers to teach myth as myth, without demythologizing, he can apply the principle of interpretation which Crombie suggests as a basis for discussion. Poetry may be interpreted in the same way. But a parable often has an extra sting which other forms may lack: "Go and do likewise." It is not only an occasion for a disclosure but also for commitment.

Stories, parables, and other forms of discourse for purposes of Christian education do not exist in isolation. Ramsey provides for this indirectly with the off-hand corollary "that to understand religious language or theology we must first evoke the odd kind of situation." [38] It is not clear to me how much this involves. He places the "empirical anchorage" in "worship, wonder, awe. Without such an empirical anchorage all our theological thinking is in vain, and where there is controversy and argument we are to look for their resolution where they are fulfilled: in worship." [39]

This is one kind of situation in which discernment may be evoked, but the language of worship needs the same kind of logical analysis that Ramsey has provided for other forms of the language of faith. The unreality of worship is one of the barriers to any kind of Christian nurture for many people. Furthermore, the statement on worship does not take into account the characteristically personal and interpersonal situations to which Ramsey briefly alludes in a later article.[40] Here there needs to be an awareness of the kinds of groups that make dis-

---

[37] I. M. Crombie, "The Possibility of Theological Statements," Basil Mitchell, ed., Faith and Logic (London: George Allen & Unwin, 1957), pp. 70–71. See Christian Discourse, pp. 6–13.

[38] Religious Language, p. 47.

[39] Ibid., p. 89.

[40] Religious Studies, I (Oct. 1965), pp. 53, 57–58.

closures possible. Just as there needs to be some degree of prior awareness of God before language about God has currency, so there needs to be what Reuel L. Howe calls the "language of relationships" before words can have any currency at all.

With the emphasis on discernment and commitment, it sometimes seems that the end of Christian education is reached when a "decision for Christ" has been made. But it is Ramsey's key belief that all knowledge and education is rooted in insight, and thus the process of gaining additional knowledge is a continuous one. Therefore, Christian education needs to be implemented at all levels of thinking and action. There are five ways in which this may be done.

First, suggests Ramsey, we can speak of the "will of God" in terms of belief and action if we study how people with Christian commitment have talked. We discover that they have related themselves in several ways to their environment, taking seriously their involvement in the life around them. They found that in some cases they could not conscientiously participate, and they took the consequences. But normally they were not distinguished from other religious groups in terms of language, dress, food, or most of their customs, except for worship. Such a study of the past could lead contextually to the situation today, in terms of any key social or ethical problems. This could lead to an insight,

> using an obvious model, . . . of God speaking to us in our own day. . . . This insight (if it occurs, and it is not ours to command, but God's to give) will show itself in some decision, some forthright judgment on the particular problem or issue under examination, and any such judgment will exhibit *pro tem.* a moral or social Christian principle—here will be God's message, if we wish to continue the model. . . . But the process never ends.[41]

Second, Christian education needs to be brought into dialogue with other disciplines. Theology belongs in the realm of

---

[41] *On Being Sure in Religion*, pp. 35–36.

secular discourse, even with all of its logical oddities, for like the sciences and humanities it has its models and metaphors. If a genuine dialogue occurs, as it can at the university level, theology will learn much about the "ever-changing models of the various disciplines" and "work out appropriately new routes to God" as well as alert other disciplines to its own developments. Theology no longer dominates any other discipline, but it can point to the underlying theistic reality supporting all of them. Not only at the university level is this dialogue important, however, for it needs to go on as best it may within the framework of religious classes in schools and churches so that the student may know how he can stand as a Christian believer in a secular world.[42]

Third, and perhaps most significant as something new in Christian education, we can assist students in understanding by illuminating the strange logical forms which the language about God takes. "Those who sing: 'I love you for a hundred thousand reasons, but most of all I love you 'cos you're you' are not likely, if they are consistent, to expect religious language to be of the plain 'down to earth' kind, or likely to expect reasoning in religion to be of the 'knock-down' compelling kind." [43] We can help them to see the connections between the language of faith and the language of love, or between the language of models and the language of art, or between the various language-games that Wittgenstein mentions.

Fourth, many theological models "have been drained of their disclosure possibilities by the vast sociological, psychological, and cultural changes which separate us from the biblical, not least the Old Testament world." [44] This is probably the single most frustrating factor in the communication of the gospel. Some models have been worn thin by premature exposure to children, so that their use at a later age is ineffective; but chiefly

---

[42] *Models and Mystery*, p. 70. See also "A New Prospect for Theology," *Theology*, LXVII, No. 534 (Dec. 1964), pp. 527–33.

[43] In *Religious Education*, LX (Jan.–Feb. 1965), p. 14.

[44] Ramsey, in F. W. Dillistone, ed., *Myth and Symbol*, p. 92.

we have the problem of vast cultural changes in recent years. It is at this point, even without the help of linguistic analysis, that new models are being sought in such experiments as the coffee-house ministry,[45] jazz and folk song masses, the underground church, and new translations of religious terms. In today's world the sports car may replace the strong tower and the personnel officer may be a better symbol than the good shepherd.[46] A generation ago, a viable model was "Railways to heaven," which at least was closer to the truth than "God is my co-pilot." Current folk songs are loaded with models that speak to the younger generation, often with pathos and hope that match the psalms. Such new models, drawn from relevant experience in today's world, come from words that reflect new ideals and fervent hopes and have a basis in fact, but they need to be qualified so that they are never reducible to picture models.[47]

A fifth and final point made by Ramsey is that "if there is to be any religious education at all, there must be religious situations for children to explore." Such an experience as "basic trust," for example, is essential, and as part of it there needs to be appropriate language interacting with the experience. Except for worship, basic religious situations reside in secular experience, in terms of issues that are faced and relationships that are both nourishing and nurturing. To relate daily experience to Christian faith is not easy. It may involve both increased sensitivity and hard thinking. And why should not hard thinking be as essential to religion as to mathematics? [48]

Bishop Ramsey, then, has led us to a deeper appreciation of the key to understanding religious language in terms of disclosure and commitment, of models and qualifiers, and of logically odd arrangements of ordinary language.

---

[45] See John D. Perry, Jr., *The Coffee House Ministry* (Richmond: John Knox Press, 1966).

[46] See Carl F. Burke, *God Is for Real, Man* (New York: Association Press, 1966), p. 39.

[47] See *Myth and Symbol*, p. 96.

[48] See I. T. Ramsey, "The Plowden Report," *Learning for Living*, VI (May 1967), pp. 22–25.

VI. THE LANGUAGE
OF THE HEART

Many of the ideas which have been reworked in terms of logical analysis are not new. The recasting has been helpful, but older theories derived from philosophical and literary studies often provide parallels. In this chapter, we will turn to two men, Horace Bushnell, who lived in the last century in Connecticut, and Francis H. Drinkwater, a contemporary English Roman Catholic. They have similar positions and agree on the phrase which is the title for this chapter, "The Language of the Heart."

Horace Bushnell is best known for *Christian Nurture,* written in 1847, dealing with many aspects of the Christian education of children.[1] But in his own time, as a pastor in Hartford, he was in the midst of theological controversies in which he

---

[1] Bushnell's first essays and defenses appeared in 1847. The book as we now know it, considerably enlarged by later essays, appeared in 1861, and the latest edition with introductions by Williston Walker and Luther A. Weigle appeared in 1947. See *Christian Nurture* (New Haven, Conn.: Yale University Press, 1947). A selection of Bushnell's writings is conveniently available in H. Shelton Smith, ed., *Horace Bushnell* (New York: Oxford University Press, 1965).

demonstrated an originality of thought and a devotion to Christian living that are equally significant for our purposes, particularly his theory of knowledge and his theory of religious language.

Although Bushnell did not develop a full theory of religious knowledge, it is clear that he combined views of intuition and reason in a way not greatly different from the position of I. T. Ramsey. His thinking in this regard was influenced by Samuel Coleridge and Victor Cousin as well as the Puritan tradition exemplified by Jonathan Edwards. From Coleridge he derived a view of the necessity of religious intuition as a basis for belief. From Cousin he adopted the view that belief in God is necessary because human thinking cannot avoid ultimate reality. Cousin expounded a "primitive spontaneity" or "intuitive reason" upon which reflection depends. From Jonathan Edwards Bushnell accepted the doctrine of "the sense of the heart." No matter how sound a man's rational thinking may be, there must be an immediate intuition of God for his awareness to "come alive."

Knowing about God, said Bushnell, is not enough, for it is too impersonal and distant. There "is knowing God within, even as we know ourselves." This knowledge is such "that there is no language in it, no thought, no act of judgment or opinion, you simply have a self-feeling that is intuitive and direct." [2] This is the work of the Holy Spirit. Bushnell did not come to this conclusion easily, for he went through several crises in his own understanding of Christianity, each time with a renewed intuition of the presence of God or the living Christ.

As we will see when we turn to Bushnell's theory of religious language, his mind was comprehensive. He did not trust any theology that had a limited vocabulary or that rode one idea. Language is too limited to deal adequately with truth about God, and we must use all of its richness, for truth has many sides. If we look at the history of Christian thought, we

---

[2] *Sermons on Living Subjects* (New York: Charles Scribner's Sons, 1910), p. 119; quoted by Smith, op. cit., p. 33.

discover that no theory is right, for if pressed to its logical end it distorts reality and needs to be corrected by another form of statement. Yet each theory, insofar as it is responsible, stands for some aspect of truth. If we can combine the insights of the competing parties in theological discourse, by clarifying those forms which are "repugnant" and burrowing more deeply into the conflicts, a more comprehensive view will result.[3]

DISSERTATION ON LANGUAGE

Although Bushnell claimed to be no expert on language, he had read widely and had been influenced by his teachers. Yet he was critical even of positions with which he had sympathy.[4] His "Preliminary Dissertation on the Nature of Language, as Related to Thought and Spirit" was prefaced to his theological work, *God in Christ*, as a way of assisting the reader.[5] He held to this position on language and used it in all his theological writings.

Bushnell began by proposing that we think of two men, who, having no language and having heard no words, form their own words to describe things they can point at. Thus, they are agreed on nouns as applied to things. The words are arbitrary choices. From these nouns, words are then used in adjectival ways or in ways of other parts of speech. He gives some examples:

> The word *through,* and the word *door,* when traced historically, coalesce in the same origin. Nor could anything be more natural, in stringing nouns together before any precise grammar is formed, to speak of going *door* any wall or obstacle; which, if it continued, would shortly take the word *door* into a proposition, as we actually see in the word *through.*[6]

---

[3] See H. Shelton Smith, op. cit., pp. 38, 111–12.

[4] See his criticism of Cousin, ibid., p. 112.

[5] *God in Christ* (Hartford: Brown & Parsons, 1849), pp. 9–97; reprinted almost in full in Smith, op. cit., pp. 69–105.

[6] Smith, op. cit., p. 79.

And, he suggests, is a contraction of *an-add.* "A *shine* and a *run* are names of appearances, just as a *sun* and a *river* are names of appearances. And when these names are strung together, in the use, the *sun* and the *shine,* the *river* and the *run,* the idea of subject and predicate becomes associated." [7]

This accounts, says Bushnell, for the way in which language develops at the physical level. We cannot always show how this occurred, and often the development may have moved according to various orders. But the point is that words are derived from their use to point to physical objects. Furthermore, our intellectual and spiritual vocabulary is derived from such physical roots in a second order of meaning. For example:

"The word *spirit* means, originally, *breath,* or air in motion; that being the symbol, in nature, of a power of moving unseen.

"The word *religion* is *re,* back, and *ligo,* to bind. . . .[8]

"In the same way we have *prefer,* to set before; *abstraction,* drawing apart; *reflection,* turning back . . . ; *faith,* a tie or ligature." [9]

In every language, there are words for literal use and words for figurative or analogical use. Theology belongs to the second use; theologians make a mistake when they "accept words not as signs or images, but as absolute measures and equivalents of truth; and so to run themselves, with a perfectly unsuspecting confidence, into whatever conclusions the *logical forms* of the words will carry them." [10] Like Ramsey after him, Bushnell was

---

[7] Ibid., p. 80.

[8] A difference in etymology does not spoil the illustration.

[9] Ibid., p. 78.

[10] Ibid., p. 88. Owen Barfield, supported by C. S. Lewis and E. L. Mascall, takes an opposite position, claiming that early man did not start with either the physical or the spiritual meaning of words but with both at once. See Barfield, *Poetic Diction* (New York: McGraw-Hill, 1964), pp. 72–76; C. S. Lewis, *Miracles* (London: Bles, 1947), p. 94; E. L. Mascall, *Words and Images* (London: Longmans Green & Co., 1957), p. 107. See also Ludwig Wittgenstein, *Philosophical Investigations* (2d ed.; Oxford: Basil Blackwell, and New York: Macmillan, 1958), pp. 2e–10e.

arguing for the special logical oddity of religious language.

Although words of intellect and spirit are derived from those used to point to the physical state, they do not correspond with any exactness, although there is a helpful degree of correspondence. There is a mystery in this correspondence, which is analogical and figurative and never exact. Writes Bushnell:

> Words are legitimately used as signs of thoughts to be expressed. They do not literally convey or pass over a thought out of one mind into another. . . . They are only hints, or images, held up before the mind of another, to put *him* on generating or reproducing the same thought; which he can only do as he has the same personal contents, or the generative power out of which to bring the thought required.[11]

Furthermore, Bushnell claims that such words always distort meaning, because they impute form to what has no form. Genuine thinking at this level involves poetry, allegory, and stretching of the imagination. Only a flexible vocabulary can operate effectively. But the situation is complex, for when words grow away from their roots they take on new and sometimes false meanings, which can be checked only by returning to the original meaning, which in turn is not reliable for indicating its secondary meaning.

Here is where Bushnell's theory begins to take on significance for theological discourse and communication. Because of the peculiarity of religious language, all words carry with them the danger of error or partial truth. So we need to make use of many words or figures of speech, thus insuring that clarity will increase and falsifications will cancel each other. This is where paradoxes are essential, for they guard against a simplistic use of words and logic.

Although Bushnell is critical of rationalism in theology, he does not object to the use of logic and reason to order one's thought. He writes: "After the subject matter has been gotten into propositions, and cleared, perhaps, by definition, the faculty of intuition, or insight, may be suspended, and we may go

---

[11] Ibid., p. 91.

on safely to reason upon the forms of the words themselves, or the 'analogy the words bear to each other.' " [12]

It is obvious to Bushnell that creeds and catechisms do not provide dogmatic certainty. If we are able to look beneath the surface of the events that led to their formulations, we will find an element of truth in all of them, although they give the impression of diversity. If creeds are to be retained, we should assent to as many as possible and let them qualify each other.[13] Such a view emphasizes the tentativeness of theology.

Bushnell spoke against imaginative speculation, although some of his own flights of imagination articulated doctrine in a meaningful way. But at the same time, he was suspicious of all systems as such. If this approach to language is accepted, said Bushnell, "the scriptures will be more studied than they have been, and in a different manner—not as a magazine of propositions and mere dialectic entities, but as inspirations and poetic forms of life. . . . We shall seem to understand less, and shall actually receive more." [14] This presupposes a mystic element in life.

The Bible supports such a view, for it contains not only poetry but much that is like poetry in its historical accounts. Christ gave forth utterances, says Bushnell, "in living symbols, without definitions, without *proving* it, . . . well understanding that truth is that which shines in its own evidence, that which *finds* us, to use an admirable expression of Coleridge, and thus enters into us." [15] Men speak of being gripped or grasped by truth or by God; they are overcome or overwhelmed; they are loved. When the "light dawns," it is a revelation or a disclosure from the outside. Religious language points beyond the self.

Thus far, we have looked at Bushnell's theory of language as a help in communication, especially in theological discourse.

---

[12] Ibid., p. 95.
[13] Ibid., p. 101.
[14] Ibid., p. 103.
[15] Ibid., p. 98.

There is one other factor which characterizes language and ties in with his theory of Christian nurture. A person's use of words has significance and power which are individualized and personalized, says Bushnell, "whether it be the rhythm, the collocations, the cadences, or the internal ideas, it may be impossible to guess. But his language is his own, and there is some chemistry of life in it that belongs only to him, as does the vital chemistry of his body." [16] The person who speaks is as much a part of the communication process as the words that are used. Jesus' words, for example, carried a greater degree of significance because he "spoke with authority." What is communicated, therefore, not only points and shows but in an important manner reveals the hidden nature of the speaker or writer.

Certainly the proper use of words is not enough to provide Christian education. As Bushnell remarks, "Much of what is called Christian nurture, not only serves to make the subject of religion odious, and that, as much as we can discover, in exact proportion to the amount of religious teaching received." [17] Even before a child can use words, the gospel "beams out" from the Christian parent "as a living epistle, before it escapes from the lips, or is taught in words." [18] This development of the child, growing up as a Christian, is no automatic process. "It involves a struggle with evil, a fall and rescue." [19] There is an organic relationship between parents and children, which, when properly structured and supported by love, becomes the means of grace whereby God works within the group.

This interpersonal view of relationships, seen first within the family, applies also to life in the church and in the church school class. Not only do we learn about words by pointing to their physical origins and their secondary use in religious speaking, but we also learn about words which show us grace at work in the relationships of daily life.

---

[16] Ibid., p. 102.
[17] *Christian Nurture*, p. 11.
[18] Ibid., p. 14.
[19] Ibid., p. 15.

We turn from Bushnell to Francis H. Drinkwater. Both of them would agree with Georges Delcuve that the aim of Christian education "is to work with grace in the awakening or the increase of that faith which justifies us." [20]

Drinkwater was for many years editor of *The Sower*, a weekly magazine on Roman Catholic catechetics in England, as well as an inspector of Roman Catholic schools. He has been concerned with the use of words for the purpose of Christian education, and has been influenced by the thinking of Wordsworth and Coleridge. Thus, he comes at the problem from a perspective similar to that of Bushnell. There is, he says, a need for simplicity in Christian communication that will reach the middle and lower classes of society. These people have a limited vocabulary. They think in concrete terms. They are caught in the impersonal structures of an industrial society where they have lost touch with the simple, rustic life of their ancestors. Wordsworth, in his day, had the genius to articulate the charm of everyday life in terms of the loveliness of the world around him. He could "overcome the film of familiarity" by appealing to nature in a simple, poetic style that reached the heart.

This, of course, is no longer the case. The people are caught in a routine in which the charm of nature has been forgotten and cannot be renewed by field trips or poetry. Yet preaching at mass, storytelling, and dialogue need to reach the "heart." Drinkwater says that "if people can't see the difference between the emotions and the heart they have not even begun to understand what it is all about." [21] Like Coleridge and Bushnell, Drinkwater is thinking in terms of the total thinking, willing, loving person who is enabled to respond "with all his heart."

The trouble with so much language is that it refers to some

---

[20] Georges Delcuve, "Confirmation at the Age of Reason," Gerard S. Sloyan, ed., *Shaping the Christian Message* (New York: Macmillan, 1958), p. 281.

[21] "Using Christian Words," Sloyan, ed., op. cit., p. 271.

"substance" as the meaning of words that are meant to illuminate relationships or personal meanings. "Grace" as a theological doctrine, says Drinkwater as an example, is often interpreted as similar to some substance like bread or medicine, but "if we just said that God comes to live in our soul, and this New Life is what is meant by 'grace,' " would this not have meaning for simple people? [22]

There are, says Drinkwater, four categories of language:

1. *Scientific-difficult:* This is the language of mathematical physics or of the theology of Thomas Aquinas. It is essential for technical analysis, for scientific hypotheses, and for discussions among professionals. It is the language used for the establishment of the theological basis for Christian education.

2. *Scientific-simple:* This is the language of simplified arithmetic, of a weather report, and of the catechism. It is essential for passing on information on a non-technical and impersonal basis, but it never reaches the heart.

3. *Poetic-difficult:* This is the language of Francis Thompson in *The Hound of Heaven* or of some of the poetry of T. S. Eliot and Robert Browning. At its worst, it is like the poem of which Browning is reported to have said: "When I wrote it only God and Robert Browning knew what it meant; now, God only knows."

4. *Poetic-simple:* This is the "language of the heart." Drinkwater's example is Lincoln's Gettysburg Address. It is the language found in much of the Bible, especially the psalms, the beatitudes, and some of the parables of Jesus. Poetry is here used in the broad sense that parallels some of the logically odd qualifiers suggested by Ramsey and the combinations of words recommended by Bushnell, who also recognizes the significance of poetry. Even when a poet has been using difficult words, Drinkwater reminds us, when he wants to get to the heart he uses poetic-simple:

---

[22] Ibid., p. 273.

"Good night, sweet prince;
And flights of angels sing thee to thy rest!"

This language is so simple that every word but one is of a single syllable.[23]

"The science of theology," he writes, "must erect a lofty structure of truth expressed in scientific language upon a basis of truth expressed in non-scientific language. It is like building a mighty bridge not on solid ground, but across some wide river bed. This can be done to last, but not by any second-rate engineers in a hurry." [24] Teachers need to reverse this process. They need to be grounded in theology, even when it does not reach the heart, but they need to translate the scientific-difficult language into something more immediately meaningful. Often they are content to translate from scientific-difficult into scientific-simple, and we get a kind of catechetical teaching that is deadly, turning out parrots who can repeat formulae rather than believers who are afire with faith. It is never enough to translate scientific-difficult into scientific-simple, unless the purpose is that of analysis for those who are limited in education or in acquaintance with the field.

"Teachers with pious but second-rate minds, faced with the task of teaching the scientific-difficult jargon of seminary theology and catechisms, prove quite unequal to the task of translating it even into scientific-simple language, much less the poetic-simple." [25] We need all levels of difficulty in the use of language to do the total job, but what we usually miss out on is this key task of translation into the rich and imaginative images and idioms of poetic-simple.

Drinkwater contrasts the purposes of the basic categories of language. He writes:

There is a kind of language which can reach the heart, and another kind of language which seals off the heart as effectually

---

[23] See ibid., pp. 274–75.
[24] Ibid., p. 277.
[25] Ibid., pp. 279–80.

as trouble in the fuse box shuts off the electric current. There are times when you need to shut off the electric current, for repairs or tests or some such reason, but you don't expect any light or heat during these circumstances.[26]

What Drinkwater has in focus is one specific purpose of Christian education: to evoke light and heat. Amos Wilder puts it this way: The gospel's "poem forms . . . focus upon the heart and its ultimate response to God. . . . Plastic and rhythmic language must be called forth to convey this level of experience." [27] Ian T. Ramsey, recognizing that not all poetic or logically odd language is necessarily religious, reminds all teachers that "a useful antidote for straightforward language might be found in suitable doses of poetry or greater familiarity with the curiously odd words thrown up in scientific theories." [28]

Is this sufficient? Or do we need to emphasize the point that there is a basis for belief that may be expressed in more technical language, as Drinkwater suggests in his bridge-building illustration? Ronald Hepburn warns that the analogy between poetry and theology

> is fruitful but dangerous when rashly invoked. To make effective use of it, a theologian must know something of how the language of poetry differs from that of prose description; he must come to know in detail what he is claiming when he says that such and such a biblical narrative is "imaginatively true," "a profound myth," "more than historical fact," or when he claims an affinity between the poet and the prophet. . . . The language of poetry . . . still cannot by itself lead to a defensible apologetic.[29]

---

[26] Ibid., p. 271.

[27] *The Language of the Gospels: Early Christian Rhetoric* (New York: Harper & Row, 1964), p. 98.

[28] *Religious Language* (London: SCM Press, 1957; Macmillan Paperback, 1963), p. 48.

[29] "Poetry and Religious Belief," Alasdair MacIntyre, ed., *Metaphysical Beliefs* (London: SCM Press, 1957), p. 165.

Drinkwater does not deal with this issue of apologetics. Ramsey, however, believes that logically odd phrases that lead to disclosures can be related to an underlying reality tested by "empirical fit" and speaks of the "empirical anchor" of worship. I doubt if this would satisfy Hepburn, but the evidence from Northrop, Hartshorne, and Whitehead (chapter 3) provides a broader empirical and rational base. Hepburn says that "the symbolic vessel requires a nonsymbolic anchor," [30] and the question remains for the reader to decide whether this empirical anchor is found in the suggestions of Ramsey, Northrop, Bushnell, and others.

Drinkwater certainly does not rely on the poetic-simple for the verification of the beliefs that are to be communicated. Poetic-simple is a vehicle of language for communication so that the total person may respond. It is, in Ramsey's words, "disclosure" language, not "verification" language. The two logics, like the two language-games, are not identical.

IMPLICATIONS FOR CHRISTIAN EDUCATION

As we derive implications for Christian education from Bushnell and Drinkwater, we need to examine the meaning of "poetic," see its use in the Bible even in the narrative mode, look at some modern examples of the poetic, and then stress Bushnell's emphasis on the multiple use of words especially as they can be rooted back into the prosaic and descriptive uses. But poetic-simple is not the whole of religious communication. Drinkwater suggests ways of using the other categories of language, and it becomes clear that there are proper uses of scientific-simple, poetic-difficult, and, on a more analytical level, scientific-difficult. And all such uses of language, to be effective in the religious sense as talk about God, take us back into the issue of the experience and meaning of worship.

It appears that Ramsey, Bushnell, and Drinkwater are arguing at one level of their thought for an identical theory of the use of words for communicating in terms of "the language of

---

[30] Ibid., p. 162.

the heart." They are using "poetic" in a broad sense, as rich, concrete, image thinking. They are thinking more in terms of Jesus' parables than in terms of the psalms; more in terms of metaphors and models than in terms of hymns; more in terms of unusual picture language than in terms of *Pilgrim's Progress*; but both sides of these parallels are part of the picture. The emphasis is on avoiding straightforward, prosaic language, whether it be theological jargon or scientific description. This means avoiding scale or picture models and yet appealing to the images in the human mind. It means stories of real people and parables of imaginary people without falling into fantasy thinking. It means evoking disclosures of an objective reality in life without stimulating bigotry or fanaticism. It means sensing the "undifferentiated aesthetic continuum" without losing consciousness of God as *logos*, revealed in Jesus Christ, but probably never using such language to express it. It means the experience of the mystery of the "numinous" in worship without withdrawal from the world of the secular. It means discernment of the divine followed by commitment.

When we turn to the language of the gospel, we find this point of view confirmed. The story, the parable, the poem, the myth, and other verbal symbols are the forms of presentation. The vividness of the anecdotes, with their quick flashes into the meaning of Jesus' ministry, provides occasions for discernment and commitment. The parables, with their remarkable secular realism and their challenge to go and do likewise, assist us in gaining self-knowledge when we identify with one of the characters. The challenge of the miracles for our understanding of the meaning of Jesus' ministry forces us to see the logical oddity of their presentation. The poetry, especially in Luke, some of which is written into our traditional liturgies, challenges our imagination. Why, for example, does Bach's *Magnificat* leave out the penultimate note at a crucial point about the rich and the poor? Is music capable of the same logical improprieties as words? Those passages which many consider to be myth provide a different kind of challenge. Are they now so preposterous that Bultmann's demythologizing is the only solution? And when they have been translated into the vocabulary of existentialism, are we helped or hindered? The language of "authentic existence" may pose for some the kind of logical oddity that evokes a disclosure.

Furthermore, all of these examples suggest the narrative mode which is also the key to understanding the Old Testament. There are those who claim that the basic understanding of any passage comes from identifying with one of the characters and therefore appropriating the revelation presumed to be present. The teacher is faced with the problem of reading or retelling the story in such a way that for that age-level some degree of appropriation is possible, for otherwise no disclosure could be evoked. To tell a story so that the "light dawns" and the "ice breaks" usually means using the "language of the heart." This is easier to state than it is to practice. Often the teacher not only finds it difficult to translate the story properly for the age-level, but he is unable to see the point himself. Good techniques of storytelling are not sufficient to overcome the basic handicap of lack of insight. Many times, the approach involves telling two stories, so that the biblical and the modern stories overlap and interpenetrate each other, and in the intermingling of the two stories the "light dawns." Just as a metaphor involves the mixture of two different images, so a mingling of stories may provide a disclosure situation. This is particularly true in an age when the biblical stories reflect either an irrelevant culture or an irrelevant historical period, as they do for most Westerners today. If the students have knowledge of a fund of biblical stories, it may be possible to tell a modern parallel and let them make the identification of the biblical story that is intended, thus bringing the biblical insight into their own span of attention through their own efforts. If we can bring the stories of our own lives together with Christian stories, it may lead to an increase in both self-awareness and in discernment of God in our midst.

Poetry as such has a large part to play in telling of the

meaning of Christianity. Children are capable of writing and understanding simple poetry. Here is a sample of the writing of a boy in the tenth grade (fourth form in England):

> O God, tell me the reason why
> Man goes soaring in the sky?
> Why does the world go round and round?
> Why does it not go up and down?
> Would it wreck the eternal plan
> If I should have an extra hand?
> Why is the sky so blue?
> Is it a freak, or because of you?
> I wish I knew one way or the other
> If every man was my brother.
> —Christopher Young [31]

A boy a year older catches something of the paradox of living in today's world, and the oddities face us with the possibility of a new discernment:

> Someone dropped a bomb somewhere!
> Well it's not on me—I don't care.
> But it missed its target flare
> And rendered with its napalm a village bare.
>
> The poor village worker perplexed by the scream
> Of engines looked above and saw his flying doom.
> With a blinding liberation flash and the flow
> Of jelly petrol his body was now a charred mass.
>
> But the preacher said, "The Lord is my Shepherd,
> I shall not want . . ." as his and another hundred
> Bodies were pushed into a grave, like a herd,
> With a sprinkle of lime for their coffins.
> —Thomas Stacey [32]

Like the psalms, the poetry of modern youth, to the accompaniment of a guitar rather than a harp, expresses the hopes and fears, the realities and the aspirations, the discernment and com-

---

[31] Quoted by R. W. Street, "The Use of Poetry in Religious Education," *Learning for Living*, VIII (Mar. 1969), p. 12.
[32] Ibid., p. 12.

mitment which they do not often find in more traditional forms of creed and worship. It is no accident that religious themes pervade many of the folk songs of the younger generation.

Those who have seen a performance of *A Man Dies*, a mime passion drama by Ernest Marvin developed by teenagers in Bristol, England, with its dancing and its music, realize that the message comes through most strongly in the words of its songs. The music is rhythmic in a mixture of the jazz and folk song idioms, and the words crowd into the consciousness with their power. This is especially true of the song which reoccurs with different words throughout the play:

> Gentle Christ, wise and good,
> We nailed him to a cross of wood.
> The Son of God, he lived to save,
> In borrowed stable and borrowed grave.
> When he walked into the shopping street
> We threw spring flowers before his feet,
> Glad to get an excuse to shout,
> No need to worry what you shout about.
>   Gentle Christ. . . .
> Soldiers came at Pilate's call
> Led him into the common hall,
> Took sharp thorns and made a crown,
> Dressed him in a scarlet gown.
>   Gentle Christ. . . .
> At last they came to the hanging place
> A hill we call the Eyeless Face,
> They gave him drugs to kill the pain,
> He pushed the cup away again.
>   Gentle Christ. . . .[33]

As the words continue, sung to a haunting tune with a beguine beat, the message comes through so that the light may dawn for those who would not hear the story in any other form, and it comes with renewed power to those who already accept

---

[33] © Copyright by Ivy Music Limited, London. Reproduced by permission.

the power of the death and resurrection of Jesus Christ.

Bushnell and Drinkwater provide another insight which may be interpreted in terms of Drinkwater's poetic-simple. The richness of Christian imagery demands a plurality of models and words. If we can increase the number of models and qualifiers, and if we can find synonyms for key words, somewhere along the line there may be a glimmer of light or a thawing of the ice. The New Testament is particularly helpful, for in the attempt to understand the meaning of Jesus we find a total of forty-two names, many of which have currency in today's world, and in the search for images of the church, we find ninety-six, some of which still have meaning.[34] When we talk about God, the concepts are less frequent, but the Old Testament provides four names and avoids the basic one, YHWH, because it is too holy to speak. There is the question of whether God is a name or not, or if it has the same oddity as the tautology "I am I."

The use of poetic-simple, logically odd language is primarily for reaching the total person. Insofar as the aim of Christian teaching is to evoke disclosures and commitment, this is the kind of language which our logical mapping of religious discourse requires. We shall see in the next chapter that we also need to incorporate the performative language of self-involvement. But the purpose of Christian education is not exhausted at this point.

Briefly, let us look at Drinkwater's categories of language again. His emphasis on "the language of the heart" and the "poetic-simple" is in terms of unsophisticated and uneducated people, who might find other forms of language extremely difficult. But even the uneducated ask intelligent questions, involving analysis and criticism. Therefore, it seems to me that if there is to be dialogue of any sort, it is essential that we use crit-

---

[34] See Vincent Taylor, *The Names of Jesus* (New York: St. Martin's Press, 1953); Paul S. Minear, *Images of the Church in the New Testament* (Philadelphia: Westminster Press, 1960). A theological wordbook for seventh grade and up incorporating some of these ideas is found in *More than Words* (New York: Seabury Press, 1955, 1958).

ical tools in as simple a way as possible. This is not a justification of theological jargon, but of the use of what Drinkwater calls scientific-simple as a basis for reasoning, analysis, and explanation. The problem arises when the conventional terms, however simple, have lost their meaning and their power to communicate; then we need to search for new words or find new referrals for the old ones.

My guess is that we need to do a great deal more with this kind of simple language. Here again we may be helped by Bushnell's suggestion that spiritual words have physical roots. There are secular references for most words used religiously. A boy objected to the use of "conversion" and "redemption" in church, for, as he said, "conversion and redemption are banking terms." If a class would take a number of such scientific-simple terms and compare their secular and religious uses, such words might come alive, especially when logically odd qualifiers are added. The search for synonyms is also worthwhile. For example, a class could take faith and its synonyms and find current secular and religious meanings: faith-decision-trust-commitment-belief *in* (not *that*).

The other categories of language have their value for Christian education. There are some who will want to move beyond the poetic-simple to the poetic-difficult. They can do this without going outside the Bible, especially in some of the more complicated psalms or difficult selections from the prophets. They may wish to delve into the literature of great poetry. Any stimulus to the imagination is likely to increase religious insight, and it is a mistake to assume that all disclosures can be reduced to poetic-simple without the danger of some loss of meaning. Isaiah 55, for example, is a mixture of poetic-simple and poetic-difficult, and may be understood at varying levels of meaning.

Furthermore, there are those who want to think analytically about religion. Some such students are taking university courses in religious studies, but others are those in our congregations who are capable of what Piaget calls "formal operational" thinking. They may be teenagers or adults. The controversies over John A. T. Robinson's *Honest to God* and the "death of God" debates surprised many educators and clergy who did not believe that lay people would discuss theological issues at this level. Here, then, is the point at which scientific-difficult language enters the picture at the parish and Sunday school level as well as at the college and university level. It has been said that many clergy overrate their parishioner's information and underrate their intelligence. This, I think, is often true. The problem is to provide situations in which the questions they are capable of asking may be met with honesty and in a language they are capable of using. Even the careful distinction of the various language-games may be one of the most valuable of all exercises in religious thinking, as I hope this book demonstrates.

There is one more issue coming from the Bushnell and Drinkwater contributions to our thinking. I suppose that the gospel may be heard in any situation, but Ramsey suggests that the situation in which the oddity of the language fits must also be evoked, and he suggests worship as the empirical anchor. Bushnell agrees that worship provides the framework, but he also insists that nurturing occurs within the organic unity of the family. Reuel L. Howe indicates that words have currency only when they point to previous experience in interpersonal relations. Love, for example, is not likely to be interpreted adequately by a person who has never known love from his parents; trust is meaningless to those who never have had the experience of basic trust; faith is an impossibility for those whose faith in other people has been destroyed. Religious words are influential when the person using them stands behind them, guaranteeing them not only by a sense of conviction but by an integrity of action (as is made abundantly clear in the letter of James). This suggests that there is more to the language of faith than an appeal to the "language of the heart," important as this is. The opposite point is not to be neglected: words have power to change the human situation, for they have performative value. We will look at this topic in the next chapter.

VII. SELF-INVOLVING LANGUAGE

When one examines how language is used, it is clear that God-talk goes on and that for many people it has meaning. However, very little talk about God is possible when one is limited to descriptive language and assertions that can be empirically validated. Most religious language makes use of other categories, and it is important to know which language-game one is using and how language-games may be mixed. The word God is the key in all religious language, although phrases about him and his actions are logically odd, and we need to make use of models and qualifiers in prolific abundance if we are to provide those situations in which may be evoked disclosures leading to commitment. Although many categories of language may be used in teaching about religion, the use of poetic-simple is essential when one is seeking the possibility of new insights leading to faith.

When one speaks of commitment, however, he is led into the performative language of self-involvement.

Donald Evans writes that many utterances are neutral, impersonal, and descriptive.[1] Other utterances involve the self. If I say, "Mary is his wife," I am not necessarily involved in the relationship. In saying, "Thank you for your graciousness," I imply that I am grateful. Language is used to *do* things. Even if I was insincere, I *committed* myself to action and *implied* an attitude.

Such self-involving language is a species of *performative* language. When I say, "I submit" or "thank" or "appoint" or "judge," I am doing something, performing a speech-act. What I say is neither true nor false insofar as it is a performative, although what I say is liable to infelicities. My statement may misfire because I fail to carry through, or I am not in a position to act it out, or I make a mistake.

The self-involving performatives noted by Evans belong to two classes: Commissives and Behabitives. Commissives involve a more than verbal commitment ("promise," "pledge," "covenant," "submit," "threaten," etc.). Behabitives have to do with social behavior and imply attitudes ("thank," "praise," "apologize," "blame," etc.). Performatives need not be explicit. I can promise without using the word promise and thank without saying "thank" and worship without saying "worship." Other words, in a given context, may have the same performative force.

Evans distinguishes between the performative use of words and the causal use. The latter is not part of the meaning of the utterance but has to do with its influence on people. For example, I may evoke feelings of gratitude by saying, "Thanks be

---

[1] See *The Logic of Self-Involvement* (London: SCM Press, 1963; New York: Herder & Herder, 1969). Evans builds on the theories of J. L. Austin as found in his posthumous books: J. O. Urmson and G. J. Warnock, eds., *Philosophical Papers* (London: Oxford University Press, 1961); J. O. Urmson, ed., *How to Do Things with Words* (London: Oxford University Press, 1962); G. J. Warnock, ed., *Sense and Sensibilia* (London: Oxford University Press, 1963).

to God." The thanking is performative, but the gratitude evoked is causal.

A third use of language is the expression of feelings. Evans includes "expressive" language as a form of self-involving language. Such utterances may also express attitudes, which include being for or against someone or something. Sometimes they are strongly judgmental, including statements or implications of either opinion or value. Attitudes are relational; the expression of an attitude involves one in his relationship to another.

ONLOOKS

Some attitudes are what Evans calls "onlooks." He writes:

> I have coined the word onlook as a substantive for what it is to "look on x as y." It is necessary to coin a word, for no existing word is quite appropriate. The word view would be misleading, since it is so close to "opinion," especially in its plural form, "my views concerning x." The word conception is a little too intellectual; and like "outlook" and "perspective," it lacks the element of commitment, and is too vague.[2]

Evans provides some examples that may help to make clear what he means:

> I look on God as an all-knowing Judge to be feared (or as a trustworthy Shepherd who guides me along life's way, or as a loving Father who yearns for the return of his children). . . .
> I look on my life as a game (or as a struggle, a search, a voyage, a pilgrimage, a dream, or a drama). . . .
> I look on my work as a way of making money, no more (or as one reason for living, or as my calling from God).[3]

In these onlooks there is a commissive element, for they involve policy or intention or at least a minimum of activity. There is self-involvement. There is a degree of autobiography. They take a stand. They include judgments or verdicts, for

---

[2] Evans, op. cit., p. 125.
[3] Ibid., p. 125.

often one is ascribing status, function, or role, even though this may be only a private opinion. They may express a world view. They are expressive of feelings or attitudes. They may evoke or cause a response. These are the common features of onlooks.

Onlooks may be literal or nonliteral. When I say, "I look on Mary as a sister," this is nonliteral. If I say, "I look on the vicar as my shepherd," the onlook is parabolic, and if I say, "I look on alcoholism as a disease," it is analogical. This is the point at which I can make a religious statement, "I look on God as a Father."

This leads to the distinction Evans makes between self-involving and rapportive utterances. The former are utterances in or through which one does something. The latter are those which are understood only to the extent to which one has an affinity or rapport with what the utterance is about. All expressions of onlook are self-involving and some also are rapportive. All expressions of religious onlook are rapportive. When a person tries to understand someone of another culture, or a genius, or even a younger or older person, he has difficulty; his understanding is limited both by his own conception of what actions are intelligible and by his inability to share the other's views. An utterance is classified as rapportive in terms of "conditions of understanding." [4]

This emphasis on rapportive utterances leads Evans to a distinction between secular-moral and religious language which he illustrates as follows:

> I look on every human being as a person. By "person" I do not mean merely "human being." What I mean is this: In every person there is something which claims my concern, reverence, personal involvement and acknowledgment of value—my "*agape*.". . . This attitude does not depend on his particular, observable qualities. A person is a being *such that* "*agape*" is the appropriate attitude. [5]

---

[4] See ibid., pp. 104–5, 110–13.
[5] Ibid., p. 134.

As one comes to the conviction that he is in rapport with God, he looks on God as transcendent and understands that God requires unlimited submission, unlimited trust, unlimited awe, and unlimited openness.[6] To express this, he uses transcendental parabolic onlooks, involving him in worship by which he acknowledges the glory and faithfulness of God. These parables concerning God have to do with what we can see in the world, with historical events, and with the heavens which "declare the glory of God."

There is usually some authority behind one's religious onlook. It may be a creed, a church, or a person whose judgment is considered sound. Some believe that their assertions reflect a divine onlook. Others are more pragmatic, and accept as their onlook whatever facilitates their relationship with God. There is a sense in which one "makes it true for himself" by living out the onlook in his daily life, and he is persuaded that "a *hidden influence enables* him to act in accordance with it."[7]

Evans quotes Herbert Butterfield, who with a different vocabulary says very much the same thing:

> Nobody can pretend to *see* the meaning of this human drama *as* a god might see it. . . . What one acquires is a *vision for working purposes in the world,* and one gains it by *adopting* an *attitude,* assuming a certain *role* within the drama itself . . . a mission which, though *prescribed by God,* must be accepted as self-assumed. . . . Ultimately our interpretation of the whole human drama depends on an ultimately personal decision concerning the part that we mean to play in it.[8]

We move from a minimal knowledge that God is to an acknowledgment of him in worship and a way of life to knowing God in acquaintance, says Evans.[9] It is this process which makes

[6] See ibid., pp. 224–25.

[7] Ibid., pp. 255–56.

[8] Ibid., p. 141. Quoted from *Christianity and History* (New York: Charles Scribner's Sons, 1949), p. 86. Evans supplies the italics to make clear the correspondence of ideas.

[9] See ibid., p. 200.

religious language essential, and to understand the process we need to understand how religious language works. *Words do things.* They express onlooks which are self-involving and include attitudes and commitment. Of course, men may be insincere, and hypocrisy is closely related to the misuse of performative language. Many church members have used the self-involving performative sentence, "I accept Jesus Christ as Lord and Savior," without involvement or commitment. But if there is a new onlook, its utterance in these words is a genuine performative. He may prefer to state it differently, as in "I commit myself to the ground of being," or "I look on the world and myself as under the authority of the creator-God revealed in the life, death, and resurrection of Jesus Christ." Such performative utterances may still suffer from infelicities, but obviously they have implications for behavior in the world.

Dallas M. High uses a narrower view of self-involving language than does Evans. He analyzes the *credo* form as a performative: "I believe in. . . ." This first-person use has its own logic involving the relations between the concept "person" and the concept "belief." When I say, "I believe in Jones," I am performing an act of believing. This is different from a report or observation, "You believe in Jones." "Believing is something *performed, owned,* and *claimed by, for* someone, *about* and *in* someone or something." [10] Although my believing is not infallible and is open to examination, I do not distrust my beliefs. High quotes Wittgenstein: "One can mistrust one's own sentences, but not one's own belief. If there were a verb meaning 'to believe falsely,' it would not have any significant first-person present indicative." [11]

As we have already indicated, God-talk and I-talk are closely related. High makes the same point: "The first step in making sense of religious belief-talk, and the central claim of Christian

---

[10] Dallas M. High, *Language, Persons, and Belief* (New York: Oxford University Press, 1967), p. 160.

[11] Wittgenstein, *Philosophical Investigations* (2d ed.; Oxford: Basil Blackwell, and New York: Macmillan, 1958), p. 109e.

monotheism is to observe that the word God can be quite appropriately, and, indeed biblically, modeled on the personal pronoun 'I.' " [12] So when I assert that I believe in God, I am willing to back up this statement with some kind of justification, reasons, or even empirical evidence. It is the kind of reasoning I use to back up my claim about my wife or my children, and the model comes from interpersonal relations. Yet I may claim that the use of the model does *not* mean that God is *a* person in the sense that you are *a* person, which is why all personal models for God need logically odd qualifiers.

Implications for Christian Education

As we look at the implications of self-involving language for Christian education, we need to deal with what Evans calls preunderstanding, for performatives rely on some kind of descriptive assertions about reality. There can be neutral teaching about religion, which is proper in American public schools, although it approaches a spectator sport. But the teaching of religion leads us to consider the situation and possible decision, of which rejection may be one response. Confirmation needs to be reinterpreted in terms of the significance of self-involving, rapportive, performative language. Adult education, also, must be linguistically performative, leading to action. Finally, we look at the power of words to evoke new insights and to stimulate greater loyalty and action.

Before we can turn to performative language in Christian education, some kind of preunderstanding is necessary. If a policeman says, "I arrest you for driving too fast," we can point to his authority to make an arrest, to you as the driver of the car, and to the automobile. These exist as a basis for his performative utterance. We can explain this process to the little boy in the back seat. But if I say, "I accept God's call to follow the vocation of druggist," I find that I can only point to myself. John McIntyre tells us:

---

[12] Dallas M. High, op. cit., p. 179.

In other words, a performative statement is parasitic. For this reason we can never resolve religious statements altogether into "performatives." By their very nature as "performatives" they entail for their understanding what we might call "host" statements, some at least of which must be descriptive. The linguistic analysis of religious statements cannot finally, therefore, replace the ontological enquiry concerning the descriptive account of the contextual framework of the performatives.[13]

The word parasitic means, I presume, to live off another. McIntyre says that a "host" statement must be strong enough to carry its parasites. Every performative statement presupposes at least a minimal knowledge on which it is based. Evans is content to leave it at this. In saying, "I acknowledge God as Lord," I presuppose that there is a God, but my acknowledgment takes me into the self-involving language that completes my picture of him through parabolic onlooks. Parables concerning God are connected with observable events and people, but the onlook points to God's hiddenness.[14]

In Christian education, therefore, we can do little about self-involvement and performatives until there is some empirical anchor. Discernment or disclosure, in Ramsey's terms, is prior to commitment. Yet if teaching is mostly on the level of descriptive, neutral, and nonself-involving discourse, how can the student find in this a basis for a response that is self-involving in terms of behavior and commitment? Evans does not provide a solution to this problem.

The problem is easy to see. We have tools of discourse, mostly in descriptive terms, derived from scripture, tradition, and modern situations. We may use various literary forms in order to present and clarify the beliefs of the churches. Even

---

[13] From *The Shape of Christology*, by John McIntyre, pp. 164–65. Published in the U.S.A. by the Westminster Press, 1966. © SCM Press, 1966. Used by permission.

[14] See Evans, op. cit., pp. 223–27; also Evans' essay, "Differences Between Scientific and Religious Assertions," Ian G. Barbour, ed., *Science and Religion* (New York: Harper & Row, 1968), pp. 101–33.

the indifferent student may participate in God-talk at this level, for it is safe. In worship, where the language tends to be self-involving, he can remain at the spectator level. Instead of worship being an "empirical anchor," the only response is a surface one or is negative. As Bushnell saw, merely to increase teaching at this level adds to the resistance of the pupil.

Such neutral teaching may be proper in the schools, where teaching *about* religion in an objective fashion is the norm. But there is a large gap between such purposes of a secular school and the primary goal of Christian education. The language of the Christian faith, like the language of friendship, is meant to be performative, in terms of trust, decision, commitment, followed by behavior in both words and deeds.

This means that we need to look again at the educational implications of the suggestions of Ramsey, Bushnell, and Drinkwater. Language may be used in such a way that a disclosure may be evoked, a discernment may occur, or the imagination may be stirred. If the "light dawns" and the "ice breaks," we have a basis both for "belief that" and "acknowledgment of" which is open to analysis and checking for "empirical fit," and this can lead to commitment. The language used for such teaching is at least indirectly causal.

If the response we hope for is to come, the self-involvement must be linguistic and more. This suggests that the conditions of social learning must be such that the situation is suitable for the logically odd, poetic use of and exchange of stories to illuminate the situation. It means that what has been called "an atmosphere in which grace flourishes" must predate the language used. This places the responsibility on the teacher and the class, as reflecting the larger life of the congregation, to create the kind of interpersonal relationships in which mutual trust is possible. When anyone in a class is treated as a means or a thing, as a bag to be filled with factual knowledge that can be dumped out for examination, there is no starting point for self-involving language. When each one is treated as a person, to be respected and listened to, to be given an opportunity to tell his story as he sees it, to respond to the story of the gospel if he wishes, there may be a situation in which both existential and linguistic self-involvement may be evoked.

Of course, any situation leads to performative language. If I say, "I reject all that stuff you have been trying to put into my head," it is a strong negative judgment which is nonself-involving. If I say, "All that information about Jesus Christ leaves me cold," I am making a statement that is autobiographical and implies a negative performative. If I say, after months of struggle with an issue, "Now I see the light; this is what you have been saying all along, and I couldn't get it," I am making an autobiographical report that includes two levels of performative, negative and positive. If we have been using many models and qualifiers, many parables, many words employing the richness of the performatives of the biblical onlook of our teaching, listening within the dialogue to whatever the students have to say, perhaps there will be moments of discernment, but this is not guaranteed by either the content or the method.

The problem involves more than the situation and the language. We are dealing with growing persons who develop new capacities for insight, discernment and commitment from day to day. For example, if we take confirmation or declaration of faith as in some degree requiring the capacity to understand, to acknowledge, to decide, and to make a commitment, we need to reconsider the age at which this can occur in the light of the findings of developmental psychology. The current practice ranges all the way from seven to eighteen years among the major denominations. For some it is the precondition for receiving Holy Communion, for others the First Communion is prior to confirmation. In the Orthodox tradition, baptism, chrism, and Holy Communion may be given to infants. If it is to be a childhood decision, with limitations on the significance of both the event and the decision, we may settle for the ages between seven and twelve. If we believe that the adolescent is seeking to stand on his own feet and identify with adults and that the church can provide an environment in which he is treated as an adult, we may place confirmation between the ages of twelve and fifteen. If we are concerned with the identity crisis, with the development of the attitude of basic trust, with the acceptance of adult responsibility within the congregation and in the world, the proper age for confirmation should be not earlier than eighteen or the school-leaving age.[15] If confirmation is based on the expectation of a full-fledged self-involving performative, based on judgment, behávior, and faith, including the expression of a biblical onlook centered in Jesus Christ, as our rituals indicate, then it is sheer hypocrisy to expect this to be a possibility prior to eighteen. If young people leave school at eighteen, if men may be drafted at eighteen, if girls may marry without parental consent at eighteen, if young people can vote at twenty-one, society is providing for self-involving performatives at an age when they have significance, meaning, and effective expression.

Even if there is agreement on a later age, confirmation poses another problem. Walter Neidhart cites the situation in Switzerland, where, at the suggestion of Karl Barth, the Apostles' Creed is used at confirmation, and many of the confirmands either move their lips silently or keep quiet and the congregation, not being used to this creed, does not recite it either. The ceremony becomes an empty one for all. Some pastors have reacted by eliminating any declaration of faith or vow. The words used in traditional forms have become meaningless and have no performative value, or, if they have, it is open to question whether the evidence for their effectiveness can be found in church attendance or some kind of social action. Neidhart concludes that as long as confirmation is "closely connected with social prestige, this period of life is certainly not the most fa-

---

[15] See *Religious Education*, LVIII (Sept.–Oct. 1963), pp. 411–42, and LX (July–Aug. 1965), pp. 290–302, for two symposia on "The Proper Age for a Declaration of Faith." See also W. Kent Gilbert, ed., *Confirmation and Education* (Philadelphia: Fortress Press, 1969) and *Confirmation Crisis* (New York: Seabury Press, 1968), especially F. J. Warnecke, "A Bishop Proposes," pp. 134–43.

vorable for a public declaration of faith and the ceremony related to it should rather remain without a vow." [16] Thus, we end with a nonself-involving and meaningless religious ritual.

Russell Becker suggests that there must be enough instruction prior to confirmation so that the ceremony is a performative, and that afterward education through small groups can reinforce both understanding and commitment as one moves toward maturity.[17] This leads directly into a new level of training which is essential for the churches: lay training. Confirmation would become, as Bishop Warnecke suggests, "commissioning of the layman for his ministry in God's world. It would be a commitment to the process of becoming, not a status quo membership." [18]

The adult Christian, no matter what the degree of his psychological or spiritual maturity and commitment, needs education in terms of increased understanding and strengthened performatives at and beyond the level of language. He needs to see the significance of self-involving language as he makes judgments about God, the world, and other people, as he acts in various ways as a Christian in society, and as he expresses his commitment in word and action. For many, this process begins with a deepening of understanding of a Christian or biblical onlook (which may still reflect his childhood onlook). This is why theological investigation and reflection, insofar as such endeavors are relevant to the situation, are absolutely essential; one learns to think theologically about the meaning of events in his daily life, to look on the world with all its difficulties and problems as God's world, to look on the work of Christ at least in Ramsey's minimum statement ("God did something through Jesus Christ"), and then to respond in terms of his developing onlook. Thus, he may be led to grasp what responsible Christian behavior is for him in his work, his home, his community, and his nation. He looks on the church, with the help of bibli-

---

16 *Religious Education*, LX (July–Aug. 1965), p. 297.

17 Ibid., pp. 292–94.

18 *Confirmation Crisis*, p. 139.

cal images, as a community of the Holy Spirit in the world rather than as a withdrawn pietistic communal group. Hopefully, he looks on worship as the "empirical anchor," the source of indwelling strength, and the expression of his onlook toward God and man.

As we have examined the self-involving language of performatives and the significance of onlooks, our analysis has opened up another channel of Christian education. When a person uses such language, his assertions do things, provided that they are not misplaced and do not misfire. Words also have causal use. They not only reflect our experiences, relationships, and attitudes, they also have the power to change one's onlooks. Words have changed the course of men's lives and of history. Great preaching has been the means of disclosure and commitment. Great teaching, especially when it operates within an atmosphere in which logically odd situations are evoked, has been the means whereby the "light has dawned" and a self-involving response in words and deeds has occurred. In Austin's phrase, when we know *How to Do Things with Words*, the emphasis is on *"do."*

The potential in Christian teaching is great, and the crime has been our failure in so many times and places to make the proper use of words. We have put great effort and devotion into using the wrong language-games. Our dry, sterile, impotent theologizing and catechizing has produced, as Drinkwater says, "neither light nor heat," and while we were talking our listeners, like Eutyches when Paul was lecturing, fell asleep. But it need not be so, if we begin to see how the imagination can create models and metaphors, can use logically odd qualifiers, can present ideas in poetic-simple language, so that new onlooks may occur. But can onlooks be changed and how? To that problem we now turn.

VIII. BLIKS AND
ONLOOKS

Our survey of self-involving performative language leads to the conclusion that what we expect to happen in Christian education may be expressed in terms of self-involvement and commitment based on a changed way of looking on God and the world. In this chapter, we examine in more detail the nature of bliks and onlooks in terms of the ways in which they may or may not be shared or changed, holding to the next chapter the issues arising from a world view or metaphysics. From the educational side, examples of possible teaching include the use of models and qualifiers in biblical and theological thinking, the use of the name of God, and the ways in which words do things. This leads to a concluding section on education as initiation as suggested by R. S. Peters.

One form of onlook is what R. M. Hare calls a blik.[1] A

---

[1] See above, chapter 2. See also R. M. Hare in Antony Flew and Alasdair MacIntyre, eds., *New Essays in Philosophical Theology*, pp. 99–103; John Wisdom, *Paradox and Discovery* (Oxford: Basil Blackwood, 1965), p. 43, for a thumbnail criticism; C. Ellis Nelson, *Where Faith Begins* (Richmond: John Knox Press, 1967), p. 9, for a strikingly similar interpretation of "presuppositions."

blik, we may recall, is a pervasive, probably unconscious attitude toward the world and is the basis for any inferences or explanations of a seemingly factual nature. Hare distinguishes between insane and sane bliks. It is important, he says, to recognize that everyone has a blik. It is deep-seated in the personality structure; it may reflect a rigid self-system developed to protect a person from uncanny feelings of anxiety, as in the theory of Harry Stack Sullivan; or it may provide a kind of security which is threatened by the challenge and risk of any kind of change, especially one provoked by the gospel. Furthermore, a blik may be irrational, psychotic, and unreachable by normal communication—and certainly unresponsive to logic.

A blik is not an assertion, not a concept, not a system of thought. It is what underlies the possibility of any kind of assertion about facts and their meanings. Hare writes: "Differences between *bliks* about the world cannot be settled by observation of what happens to the world. . . . It is by our *bliks* that we decide what is and what is not an explanation." Furthermore, because bliks are a basis for self-involving language, we care very deeply about our religious assertions. It becomes "very important to have the right *blik*." [2]

Hare also points out that people may agree about the facts and differ intensely about the interpretation:

> The facts that religious discourse deals with are perfectly ordinary empirical facts like what happens when you pray; but we are tempted to call them supernatural facts because our way of living is organized round them; they have for us value, relevance, importance, which they would not have if we were atheists.[3]

Even in the Gospels, on the basis of the same evidence, some concluded that Jesus was sent from God and others that he was a messenger from Beelzebub.

---

[2] *New Essays in Philosophical Theology*, pp. 100–101.

[3] Basil Mitchell, ed., *Faith and Logic* (London: George Allen & Unwin, 1957), pp. 189–90.

In other words, we can share a man's blik to the extent that we can talk about the same facts. But if we do not share the same meaning, argument will not really help. Perhaps, as Frederick Ferré suggests, theology for Hare is no more than "statements made in a worshipful attitude about the epistemological importance of *bliks*." [4] This provides us with a clue to the difficulties that theologians have when they attempt to enter genuine dialogue with each other, or that church school teachers face with recalcitrant students. Challenging a fixed blik may only increase resistance.

On the other hand, it may be that bliks are open to change. Bliks sympathetic to a Christian world view may be nurtured by home, church, and school, so that the person remains open to possible disclosures and commitments, as opposed to having a fixed blik resulting in a closed, rigid orthodoxy. Bliks, then, may be open or closed, strong or vulnerable, and sane or insane.

It is to be noted that bliks are deeply rooted in culture. Cultural anthropologists have discovered that the way one looks on his world is determined by cultural history, and that language cannot be simply translated without consideration of the cultural implications of seemingly identical words. As Northrop says, "It is only as different men use the same basic common concepts for describing, integrating, and anticipating the facts of their experience that they have a common culture." [5]

This can be demonstrated by observing the familiar variety of cultures within a small American town. One congregation insists on a literal interpretation of the Bible, along with a separation from most of the social activities at the country club or motion picture house. Another emphasizes an odd type of dress, marriage within the communal group, and a vocabulary akin to King James English. A third lives very much in the world, mixes with nonchurchgoers at the country club, and makes its wit-

---

[4] Frederick Ferré, *Language, Logic and God* (New York: Harper & Row, 1962), p. 131.

[5] F. S. C. Northrop, *Man, Nature and God* (New York: Pocket Books, Inc., 1962), pp. 35-36.

ness without emphasizing the differences among various groups. A fourth looks to the Vatican for many of its ideas, has recently put aside its Latin liturgy, and is beginning to use folk music in its worship. A fifth is seeking a new interpretation of black religion and is realigning itself for new approaches to civil rights.

These and other groups might be identified. They share a common heritage in the Bible, but their histories have been separated by many years of lack of contact at the religious level. If some of them come together for ecumenical dialogue, they are not sure what the others are talking about. On some issues, such as the Genesis stories, the Virgin Birth, birth control, sexual ethics, communism, the race question, the war, and many other issues, their bliks will be so evident that genuine dialogue will be impossible.

When, to this diversity of cultural conditioning and the resulting bliks among Christians, there are added the secular assumptions of the small town, the aspirations of the younger generation, and the mobility of the people, the diversity is even more obvious. The one unifying factor is that the people have been educated in an atmosphere that is not only secular but that reflects the easy assumptions of a scientific secularism, where all the answers may be found in terms of human knowledge.

If we look beyond the small town to the great urbanized centers, the diversity is multiplied. If we look beyond the cities to the nation, it is a wonder that people can operate on the same wave length, yet so pervasive is modern secularism that it has become a *lingua franca*. When we look to the wider horizons of other nations and cultures, the situation is almost overwhelming. The challenge of bliks faces us on all these levels.

An invitation to share one's blik [6] is one way to interpret Christian education. Granted Hare's use and van Buren's adaptation of it, this becomes one form of hope for change. But bliks and onlooks are closely related, and onlooks may be the basis

---

[6] See Paul M. van Buren, *The Secular Meaning of the Gospel* (New York: Macmillan, 1963), pp. 100–101.

for an approach that is more helpful for communication of a Christian understanding of life.

ONLOOKS

An onlook, says Evans, is an expression of an attitude, an assertion of a way of looking on the world of experience. In some ways it may approach the meaning of blik. Let us take the standard blik illustration: "I look on all Oxford dons as murderers." As an onlook, this statement is open to investigation. Only if, against the evidence, the student persists in his belief, would we ascribe Hare's phrase "insane blik" to him. In other words, a "sane blik" involves the kind of openness to evidence that may alter one's onlook.

If this looks too easy, however, and makes an onlook seem like an opinion based on evidence, we need to remind ourselves of some of the features of onlooks. They express commitment, for even if I have a strange belief about Oxford dons, I am committed to protect myself from them. They are autobiographical, for it is *my* way of looking and reporting. They indicate that I take up an attitude or posture toward the object of my onlook. They express a judgment or decision. They are, in short, self-involving and performative.[7]

Religious onlooks are expressed in forms of analogy and parable, says Evans. When I speak of God's glory, I am using a transcendental parabolic onlook. When I speak of his power, I am using a metaphysical onlook based on the analogy of human power. If I look on God as having his own authoritative, divine onlook, I do not assume that my onlook is identical with his. If I do move to the point at which I look on my onlook as identical with God's, I am approaching Hare's insane blik that cannot be reasoned with.[8]

The purpose of Christian discourse at one level, therefore, is to bring about a Christian or biblical onlook, for within this

---

[7] See Donald Evans, *The Logic of Self-Involvement* (London: SCM Press, 1963; New York: Herder & Herder, 1969), pp. 126–27.

[8] See ibid., pp. 254–56.

framework of fact and meaning the Christian is enabled to live in grace and faith. If the student asks why he should adopt this onlook, Evans answers: "Here the Christian will point to the Jesus of history and of Christian experience." [9] But pointing is not enough. Evans continues, "Neither nature nor Jesus provide an adequate basis for a *self-involving* confession in God the creator unless they are interpreted in terms of a complex pattern of biblical or quasi-biblical onlooks." [10]

If nothing can convince one to change his onlook, will he change it by "an act of faith"? But if he lacks a religious onlook to begin with, in whom does he place his faith? It seems to me that Evans leaves us with this dilemma: one must have a biblical onlook in order for Jesus Christ to provide a basis for self-involving language; one cannot gain this biblical onlook by exposure to God or Jesus outside this biblical onlook; therefore, unless there is already a biblical onlook there is no basis for Christian teaching.

But in Christian teaching something happens. In Evans' language, a student may say, "I never looked on religion that way before." The statement of a religious onlook may be what John Wisdom calls "attention-directing." When one looks at an abstract painting, he may be confused. As he keeps looking, his attention is directed to some of the patterns, and he begins to look on it in a different way. He points out his discovery to a friend who has said, "I don't see anything in that blob of paint," and the friend then says, "Now I see." The attention-directing leads to looking on the painting in a new way, although the facts have not changed. [11]

So also the theist and the atheist live in the same world, and as they observe the same facts, they see different patterns of meaning. The student and the Christian teacher observe the

---

[9] Ibid., p. 265.

[10] Ibid., p. 267.

[11] John Wisdom, "Gods," John Hick, ed., *Classical and Contemporary Readings in Philosophy and Religion*, pp. 423–24.

Bliks and Onlooks 131

same world, but one can lead the other to see the structure of experience in a new way.

This brings us up against the promise of the gospel that a man can become a new being in Christ. The promise of transformation, of conversion, of being reborn is at the center of the Christian tradition. It is the discovery of a sense of identity or integrity, usually involving a change of direction in one's life. It is an enabling experience, whereby one's direction, onlook, and commitment are redirected. It is the centering of one's total self in trust in the divine being. Such experiences may be as dramatic as Paul's, as simple as having one's heart "strangely warmed," as daily as the renewal of a slightly tarnished onlook at the end of the day's work.

Normally one grows up within a Christian community and family. The growing person shares the way of attending to the reality in his life in the same way as his mentors and companions. It is said, for example, that much of the racial prejudice that develops in each generation is derived by contagion from the elder generation. The attitudes of parents, for example, as Bushnell writes, in terms of "character, feelings, spirit and principles must propagate themselves" in spite of the parents' intentions or words.[12] Ideally, the children will acquire an onlook that is open toward religious faith and tentative in dogmatic statements of belief. This openness is not thought of so much as a protest against dogmatism as an insistence on the possibility of newer and richer insights and formulations of belief.

Such nurture in home and church, based on the love and acceptance of the student as he is, providing a basic structure for his life, insuring that he will be free to grow, assisting him in establishing his own authenticity, and offering him a life which shares the mystery of worship, will enable him to look on his world as God's world. This onlook, shared from the beginning of his life, may become more his own as he develops. Thus, he

---

[12] *Christian Nurture* (New Haven, Conn.: Yale University Press, 1947), p. 76.

will acquire the use of self-involving and performative language with less risk of infelicities.

The Christian onlook, which is hard to grasp from the outside, is commended by those who are concerned to live as Christians within the group. Much of this communication is in terms of the language of relationships, which may or may not be backed by words. When students are ignored, hurt, rejected, and misunderstood by those who claim to be followers of Christ, a negative onlook may begin to form. The child sees in the failure and hypocrisy of adults the misfires and abuses of performative language. But when relationships are sound, even when there are breaks in them, the healing and redeeming power of the gospel is at work strengthening faith and supporting onlooks. Such relationships provide the background for verbal teaching.

METHOD AND DISCLOSURE

We are not concerned with all the methods of Christian education but with the use of language for the nurture and changing of onlooks. We can begin to utilize at this point some of the educational insights derived from our study of language-games, the logically odd use of ordinary language, the models and qualifiers, the figurative use of seemingly descriptive words, the poetic-simple, and self-involving performatives. In genuine conversation or dialogue, for example, when trust makes listening possible, a simple confession of personal faith, an autobiographical performative statement, may be called for. In response to the questions of the learners, the teacher may join in the search by sharing the biblical onlook, which may need to be established by careful Bible study, including attention to the Bible's use of language. In examining the Gospels, the question may be opened for discussion by telling a story or recounting a parable or creating a modern myth.

For example, a group of high school students may be facing the standard but almost impossible question, "Is God good?" An affirmative is too simple and straightforward, and, as Ramsey has suggested, the reply of Christians would be that he is "infinitely good." This brings in the issue of the logically odd qualifier. God is not just "good and more," for that is not what "infinitely" means. So, if we follow Ramsey, we will start hunting for stories that may help to evoke a disclosure. Perhaps the first story is that of the tree of the knowledge of good and evil, in which there is evil in the world to be known by man. This makes possible the insight into one's own freedom to choose good or evil. The discussion at this point could move in a number of directions. One group might stay with Genesis and examine the stories of Cain and Abel, Noah, and the tower of Babel. Another might move to the analogy of father and children as found in the psalms: "As a father is kind to his children, so is the LORD kind to those who revere him (Ps. 103:13, G)," or in Jesus' teaching, "So if you, as bad as you are, know enough to give your children what is good, how much more surely will your Father in heaven give the Holy Spirit to those who ask him for it (Luke 11:13, G)." Or the questions may move toward non-man-made evil in a world where God is "infinitely good." The discovery of Job, as Walter Lippmann put it, was that "God is not like Job." [13] The qualifier "infinitely" places God's goodness beyond any simile that man may use and stretches the analogy of goodness to its furthest point where the "light might dawn." There is no pious, easy answer to the issue of God's goodness in a world where Satanic forces beyond man's power to cope are let loose. Yet Job is enabled to say:

"Lo, he will slay me; I have no hope;
Yet will I defend my ways to his face (Job 13:15, G)."

Here the integrity of Job is maintained in the face of a deity who opposes him. This is not trust in a deity who seems to do evil. Job's wife, when she saw the evidence, said:

"Do you still hold fast to your integrity?
Curse God and die! (Job 2:9, G)."

---

[13] A *Preface to Morals* (New York: Macmillan, 1929), p. 214.

His friends gave all sorts of pious but useless advice. Job, with access to the same facts, saw them in a different pattern, in which he found a basis for his own integrity and for his own understanding of the mystery of God's incomprehensible ways.

A teacher and class could stay with Job indefinitely, going beyond the text to the play *JB*, or using a passage from Isaiah to illuminate Job's point:

> "But as the heavens are higher than the earth
> So are my ways than your ways,
> And my thoughts than your thoughts (Isa. 55:9, G)."

The important point to note here is that in this analogy heaven and earth are entirely separate categories, not brought together by modern space exploration. The usage must be seen in its original context in order to have currency in today's world. If this difference is not comprehended, the Isaiah model must be discarded, for it will seem that God's goodness is only more than man's, as a space module is more competent in space than an old piston airplane, and this is not what the qualifier "infinitely" means. Perhaps by now there will be a disclosure sufficient for the students at this point in their development.

If the students are seeking still further insight, the qualified model "infinitely good" might be extended to include "infinitely powerful" and "infinitely loving." The qualifiers are essential, for God's power is not like man's power and his love is not like men's love; the analogical ascription is there, for we need to start with what we know about human power and love, but God is not like man and is not created in man's image. Perhaps the approach here is through looking on God as operating within the framework of man's freedom, and the story of the crucifixion and resurrection may lead to the discernment of God's taking on himself the consequences of man's suffering and sin. The motifs of death and new life, of being lost and found, of alienation and reconciliation may assist in the process at this point. If a disclosure occurs, there will be a changed onlook leading to self-involvement at a new level, which can be reported in performative language.

Small children have trouble with the name of God, although they sometimes have strong attachment to the name of Jesus. This difficulty with God's name was brought out in an experiment with a group of second-graders in an ecumenical setting who were being taught about the Jewish faith. Dorothy Dixon reports:

> After studying Moses' encounter with God who gave his name as Yahweh, the children seemed to enter into a personal relationship. Evidently it is difficult for a child to relate personally to the generic term God; whereas children can sense a real encounter with "Yahweh" who gives his name and who knows all his children from Abraham, Isaac, and Jacob, to Ginny, Jeff, and Bryan! Songs with "Alleluia" in them became especially meaningful as the children realized that the word means "Praise be to Yahweh!" Spontaneously in their art work the children began adding such phrases as "Yahweh, we love you" and "We will follow Yahweh." [14]

To call God "God" is like calling Jesus "god-man" or one's beloved Elizabeth "wife." No wonder that piety has addressed itself to Jesus, Mary, and the saints, preferring these genuine names to Creator, Logos, or Holy Spirit! Of course, this approach, which may be helpful at the second-grade level or which may be fanciful thinking which will not stand up, is open to question biblically. "Yahweh" is just the word that the Jews refused to pronounce because it was so holy; and they substituted various euphemisms. This difficulty, which does not have a straightforward way out, makes one point clear: we need old and new models for God in today's world.

We do not know God's name, and this is hard to explain to second-graders. As Ramsey says, "only God could know his own name. . . . The inevitable elusiveness of the divine name

---

[14] Dorothy A. Dixon, "Ecumenical Education for Second Graders," *Religious Education*, LXI (Sept.–Oct. 1966), p. 385. See Ian T. Ramsey, *Religious Language* (London: SCM Press, 1957), pp. 108–12.

is the logical safeguard against universal idolatry. . . . But YHWH witnesses to a religious situation for whose understanding we need *personal categories*." [15] Mrs. Dixon's children were right, because the use of the name Yahweh gave them a personal handle by which they could think about God, but as they grow they will be ready for the further disclosure of the mystery where all that God will say is, "I am I," which is the ultimate tautology.

Words Do Things

Words do things. They sell every kind of merchandise, often with logically odd phrases, but more often with catchwords that are easily identifiable. They are repeated ad nauseum. This use of words is effective when it is based on motivational research, is meant to overcome man's resistance and to arouse his desires, and is aimed at encouraging action. It is deep-seated enough to affect his onlooks and sometimes gets down to unconscious bliks.

This comparison is not irrelevant to our thesis. One of the most effective advertisements on television several years ago showed a girl who gets into all kinds of trouble, perils from which an escape is unlikely, and who always lands in a Dodge automobile. One's attention is caught by the humor of the odd situation. Dirty and disheveled but obviously in a good humor, she then points at the viewer and says, "The Dodge Boys want you!" So we tell our logically odd stories about Jesus who is Savior and Redeemer, and at the end we say, "Christ wants you!" Both the Dodge Corporation and the church have discovered that in many cases the viewer changes his onlook and responds with a performative, by saying that he will buy a Dodge or by acknowledging Jesus as Lord.

This performative power of words to change a person's way of thinking, by providing a new center of attention whereby the pattern of his perception of facts is changed, by stimulating a way of looking on himself and his world, by evoking a disclosure

[15] *Religious Language*, p. 112.

of meaning for his life, should never be discounted. The facts do not change! The empirical evidence is available equally to the atheist and theist, the Buddhist and Christian, the Catholic, Orthodox, Protestant, and Jew. But the onlooks differ not only in detail but in degree, and the question of truth remains as an expression of what is really there.

Direct discourse, based on the so-called facts, is never enough. Religious language has a richness that includes humor, hyperbole, fantasy, and appeals to the imagination, and yet it is grounded in reality. When Nathan told his little story about the poor man with the single lamb, which the rich man took in order to entertain a guest, David was deeply moved and became indignant, saying that the rich man should give the poor man four lambs and deserved to die. Against the background of David's sexual adventures with Bathsheba and the elimination of her husband, Uriah, Nathan's story was not objective but carried the punch line: "Thou art the man!" Here was existential self-knowledge made available, a disclosure of the meaning of the situation, and out of it came a confession and commitment by David.

This story has not lost its power or its relevance, because modern man is not different from David. He may express his attitude in terms of *Playboy* magazine, where his modern Bathsheba is found in the center foldout sheet, which provides a philosophical justification for such activity (although he would probably not resort to murder of a contemporary Uriah), or he may simply be a man who is aware of his masculine nature in terms of Jesus' words that if one looks on a woman with adultery in his intentions, he is already guilty.

When this story is placed beside that of Hosea, another disclosure may be evoked. For Hosea tells us that God is loving and forgiving, not simply in terms of the forgiving by Hosea of an erring wife, but in terms of prophecy. For it takes the story of whoredom and places it in a religious context, so that we are enabled to look on Israel (and ourselves) as a faithless wife forgiven by the Lord. Therein, we look on God in his relationship with all people, not only in Hosea's time but throughout history. Thus, we are drawn more completely into a biblical onlook.[16]

EDUCATION AS INITIATION

The concept of education presupposes that some kind of change in the student will occur. R. S. Peters speaks of education as initiation. "Education," he writes, "involves essentially processes which intentionally transmit what is valuable in an intelligible and voluntary manner and which create in the learner a desire to achieve it, this being seen as having its place along with other things in life." [17] This is something broader than instruction or training or even teaching, and may not meet all the criteria of what education is. Therefore, he prefers the term "initiation," which is a value-loaded term pointing to "worthwhile activities and modes of conduct." This is a slow process, because it includes not only knowing but doing as a goal for the student. He needs to know about Christianity, but he also must become competent as a believer. He not only must know theology, but he must also do it at his own level of competence.

Initiation then is a form of exploration, and

> great teachers are those who can conduct such a shared exploration in accordance with rigorous canons, and convey, at the same time, the contagion of a shared enterprise in which all are united by a common zeal. That is why humor is such a valuable aid to teachers; for if people can laugh together they step out of the shadows of self-reference cast by age, sex, and position. This creation of a shared experience can act as a catalyst which releases a class to unite in their common enterprise.[18]

---

[16] See ibid., pp. 112–16.

[17] "Education as Initiation," Reginald D. Archambault, ed., *Philosophical Analysis and Education* (London: Routledge & Kegan Paul, 1965), p. 102. See also R. S. Peters, *Ethics and Education* (London: George Allen & Unwin, 1966), pp. 46–88.

[18] *Philosophical Analysis and Education*, p. 107.

With this feeling of fraternity based on a common respect for persons, the class is free to explore, think, and act, and so to develop interests that are unsuspected.

Because it is a long process in which there is'much hard work, the teacher should not expect an immediate response. Each session of a class does not end with a disclosure or a commitment. Many times, students will do nothing that has any effect on their lives, nothing approaching self-involvement or performative action, either verbally or physically. As Gabriel Moran writes, "The really deep values of Christian revelation are those that emerge organically over a long period of time."[19] Premature commitment is more dangerous than no commitment. Children and young people may be said to be "on the way" and Christian maturity is a possibility only for adults. What Josef Goldbrunner calls the "theocentric crossing" is a gift of grace, when the disclosure does occur and the student responds. Slowly an onlook, autobiographical and performative, develops, and one looks on the world as God's. Such an onlook is metaphysical in its implications, and to this issue of metaphysics we now turn.

[19] Gabriel Moran, *Catechesis of Revelation* (New York: Herder & Herder, 1966), p. 125.

IX. A WORLD VIEW AND CHRISTIAN EDUCATION

We have discussed various types of language and their implications for Christian education. Each of the categories of language has its specific uses, and the problem is to be clear about which language-game one is using and to avoid improper mixing. As language leads one into theology, either through a moment of disclosure or through the adoption of a new onlook, the religious person has the problem of fitting what he comes to believe about God into a world view. His idea of God, whether as an immanent being working through natural events, a transcendent being above yet influencing events, or a transcendent-immanent God both related and not related to history, has to be placed within some kind of world view. He comes to look on God not only as a loving being but also as related in some way to the world and to the universe. Thus his theological questions become metaphysical ones as he asks about the nature of reality, of existence, of being.

The Christian is neither an expert theologian nor an expert philosopher, but as he does theology on his own terms he is covertly doing metaphysics. His view is probably like that described by van Buren: "somewhat empirical, somewhat pragmatic, somewhat relativistic, somewhat naturalistic, but also somewhat aesthetic and somewhat personalistic." [1] This is a somewhat vague and descriptive approach and should remain such even if it fails to satisfy the experts, for it is enough for most people to build on, according to van Buren.

Frederick Ferré finds this view inadequate, however, partly because it fails in its descriptive aspect and chiefly because it lacks a normative element. A descriptive metaphysics is unable to evaluate properly even a "common sense" view.[2] We need to make things comprehensible, even if we are limited in our vocabulary so that we say things obscurely through metaphors, analogies, and paradoxes.[3] "Speculative philosophy," writes Whitehead, "is the endeavor to frame a coherent, logical, necessary system of general ideas in terms of which every element in our experience can be interpreted," but they "are not dogmatic assertions of the obvious; they are tentative formulations of the ultimate generalities." [4]

Man becomes a metaphysician because he is seeking to realize his own nature as a person; he is seeking to overcome the depersonalizing that nature forces on him by interpreting the mystery at the center of all existence; [5] or as C. B. Daly puts it, "metaphysics is the 'I's' quest for the why of being and for the why of the self as the questioner of being. There are no why's in science." [6]

[1] Paul M. van Buren, "Christian Education *Post Mortem Dei*," *Religious Education*, LX (Jan.–Feb. 1965), p. 5; also *Theological Explorations* (London: SCM Press, 1968), p. 64.

[2] See Frederick Ferré, "Paul M. van Buren's A-theology of Christian Education," *Religious Education*, LX (Jan.–Feb. 1965), p. 22.

[3] See H. H. Price, H. D. Lewis, ed., *Clarity Is Not Enough*, pp. 39–40.

[4] A. N. Whitehead, *Process and Reality* (Cambridge: Cambridge University Press, 1929; New York: Macmillan, 1929), pp. 4, 12.

[5] See Ian T. Ramsey, ed., *Prospect for Metaphysics* (New York: Philosophical Library, 1961; London: George Allen & Unwin, Ltd., 1961), pp. 191, 204.

[6] C. B. Daly, ibid., p. 193; also Dallas M. High, *New Essays in Religious Language* (New York: Oxford University Press, 1969), p. 114.

The theologian and the lay person have been wary of metaphysics, the former because he is concerned with the religious dimension of life in isolation from metaphysical questions, the latter because of the technical demands for thinking on the nature of reality writ large. But the issue will not die, because the moment we begin to do theology we are involved in questions about the nature of reality. If I look on God as creator or redeemer, my onlook includes the claim to deal with reality. As Dorothy Emmet writes, "The question cannot be avoided, since religion loses its nerve when it ceases to believe that it expresses in some way truth about our relation to a reality beyond ourselves which ultimately concerns us." [7]

From the standpoint of the use of language, we can say that religious language is incipiently metaphysical language. The logic is much the same, although perhaps more generalized in metaphysics. Is there, as Ramsey indicates, "some kind of language-map by which, in some way, to understand the whole Universe"? [8] If we can locate and identify such a language map, we must use it for the proper purposes.[9]

Ramsey as usual approaches the topic from an oblique angle. He suggests that we look at some uses of language which take us beyond ordinary language. In arithmetic, we can use the concept "five" to apply to cows, fingers, balls, stars, and dumplings. Mathematics and allied sciences provide generalized theories that unite various items of experience that are otherwise diverse. The idea of gravity, for example, unites falling apples, the moon and stars, and tides. It is a subordinate or ancillary scheme that helps us bring things together. Metaphysics, says Ramsey, is like this. Logic, likewise, brings things together in a specialized language, although it touches ordinary language at vital points.

_____

[7] Dorothy Emmet, *The Nature of Metaphysical Thinking* (London: Macmillan & Co., Ltd., 1945), p. 4.

[8] *Prospect for Metaphysics*, p. 154.

[9] See Frederick Ferré, "Mapping the Logic of Models," Dallas M. High, ed., *New Essays in Religious Language*, pp. 70–71.

One illustration used by Ramsey is as old as an elementary course in theory of knowledge. Is the stick in the water "really" crooked, as it looks in the water, or straight, as it looks on dry land? Once we understand how light rays work, we can use this theory to explain how the stick may appear crooked but really be straight. We are using a special language to get at the situation which common sense acknowledges without knowing why.

Metaphysics is concerned with getting at the nature of reality, using similar specialized language-games. It "is no mere extension of ordinary language," but by its specialized function in a subordinate role intends to be "illuminative of common-sense assertions as a whole." [10] It does not replace ordinary language and it is not a higher form of scientific language. However, metaphysical language seeks to unify the logically diverse languages of science and common sense, to provide a unified view by which we look on "reality." This takes what Ramsey calls "integrative concepts." For the theist this is the concept of God. Other integrative concepts have been used in the history of philosophical thinking, but from the standpoint of religious philosophy we come back to the key word, God.

This word, says Ramsey, is modeled after the word I. There is no purely descriptive way to get at my private knowledge of myself as a person. Something more is involved, for I can "reveal" myself to another. Such a disclosure is more than descriptive analysis. Ramsey elaborates this point as follows:

> If there were no other disclosures but those around persons, we might be content with a pluralistic map; if there were no other disclosures but those reached by ethical techniques we might be believers in "Absolute Values"—ethical thinkers like Russell at the present time. But disclosures are more diverse than this, and in outline the justification for theism arises because the word God is such an admirable integrator. Disclosures can occur which do not arise around personal or moral behavior but around cosmic events or microcosmic phenomena. These can occur when we reflect on causal sequences, when we

---

[10] *Prospect for Metaphysics*, p. 159.

look at daffodils in a particular way, or penetrate into the secrets of the ocean-bed. In all such disclosures we are aware of some "other," which cannot be thought to be another "I." Such situations as these are *preeminently* those which afford the empirical basis for theism. For they connect "God" with all those features of the world that a metaphysics confined to persons or values would have to ignore. "God" can now integrate not only talk about persons and values but talk about science and perception.[11]

At this point, when Ramsey describes our talking about God, he consistently develops what he has already said in *Religious Language*, and which we evaluated in chapter 5. Such language, we recall, is logically odd and evokes disclosures. We become as certain of God as we are of ourselves, but not in terms of description.

This places metaphysics in the area of mystery. It begins with intuition, insight, disclosure, revelation, just as theology does. However, metaphysics is not satisfied with a statement of mystery. It "cannot end," says Daly, "until it has rendered such reason of that mystery that it shall not become instead absurdity. The true alternative is not mystery *or* clarity, but mystery *or* absurdity." [12]

Toward a Metaphysics

One way of starting to develop a metaphysics is to take seriously what Ramsey and Poteat say about "I" language. In other words, the model is derived from generalizing on one's own inner experience. Our own existence is the key. The experiencing person is not a substance or a thing; he is experiencing himself as relational or social, as a process that moves from past to present to future. He is related to his own body. He is affected by the complex state of his own organism. Through all the complexities of experiences, he affects his surroundings and

---

[11] Ibid., p. 173.
[12] Ibid., p. 204; High, op. cit., p. 126.

is affected by them, and he has to make decisions. He is a process of creative becoming.

One can think of God as supreme, unique, and qualitatively different from man, and yet interpret him in strict analogy with ourselves. Gone is the unrelated and nonsuffering Absolute, who is timeless and indifferent. As Schubert Ogden says:

> God is now conceived as precisely the unique or in all ways perfect instance of creative becoming, and so as the one reality which is eminently social and temporal. . . . God is related to everything. . . . He . . . is understood to be continually in process of self-creation, synthesizing in each new moment of his experience the whole of achieved actuality with the plenitude of possibility as yet unrealized.[13]

Such a deity is working for our good and is affected by what we do. His perfection does not eliminate his sharing of our suffering, his sorrow over our sin, or his joy over our turning to him. He is in our midst; he is "everywhere," says John B. Cobb, Jr., "but he is not everything. The world does not exist outside God or apart from God, but the world is not God or simply part of God. The character of the world is influenced by God, but it is not determined by him, and the world in its turn contributes novelty and richness to the divine experience."[14]

Such a concept of God, developed to technical fullness by Whitehead and adapted by others such as Ogden, Cobb, Norman Pittenger, Peter Hamilton, Daniel Day Williams, and preeminently Charles Hartshorne, is part of a metaphysical structure of thinking. The idea of God has not been tacked onto another system, whether it be Plato's, Aristotle's, or Kant's. Whitehead's metaphysics requires a dipolar concept of God, much more complex but similar to what we have described.[15]

---

[13] *The Reality of God*, p. 59.

[14] John B. Cobb, Jr., *God and the World* (Philadelphia: Westminster Press, 1969), p. 80.

[15] None of the writers cited agrees wholly with Whitehead, but he is their inspiration at many points. They more or less agree in the way they look on the universe around us, and their vision of God is built into their metaphysical thinking.

Whitehead speaks of God in two ways: in the first (primordial) he is the conceptual realization of what might be; he is the structure of possibilities; he is the eternal orderer of the world. "He is," says Whitehead, "the lure for feeling, the eternal urge of desire. His particular relevance to each creative act as it arises from its own conditioned standpoint in the world, constitutes him the initial 'object of desire' establishing the initial phase of each subjective aim." [16] In the second (consequent) way, God is sharing with creatures the power of his being, so that all increase of value in the world increases the richness of his being. He is conscious, personal, and fully actual. He has infinite patience. "He is the poet of the world, with tender patience leading it by his vision of truth, beauty, and goodness." [17]

Whitehead is protesting against some of our inherited ideas of God on both religious and metaphysical grounds. He is violently opposed to concepts of God derived from autocratic forms of government, at whose word everything began, whose rule is by divine fiat, and who is ultimately responsible for all evil and suffering. But Christianity in its original Galilean form, says Whitehead,

> does not emphasize the ruling Caesar, or the ruthless moralist, or the unmoved mover. It dwells upon the tender elements in the world, which slowly and in quietness operate by love; and it finds purpose in the present immediacy of a kingdom not of this world. Love neither rules, nor is it unmoved; also it is a little oblivious as to morals. It does not look to the future; for it finds its own reward in the immediate present.[18]

Reality finds itself transformed and "everlasting in the Being of God. In this way, the insistent craving is justified—the insistent craving that zest for existence be refreshed by the ever-present, unfading importance of our immediate actions, which perish and yet live for evermore." [19]

[16] *Process and Reality*, p. 522.
[17] Ibid., p. 526.
[18] Ibid., pp. 520–21.
[19] Ibid., p. 533.

The absolute monarch with his arbitrary control and transcendent majesty is overcome by this approach, for he has no place in a process metaphysics. But the question remains: Can a deity who is not absolute bring about the transformation of reality? [20] Is persuasion enough? Does love conquer all? If an approach that is primarily metaphysical points toward such hope, the result approximates what many consider to be the Christian hope based on some aspects of scripture, and therefore the views of Whitehead and those who seek to interpret Christianity within a similar metaphysical framework can be commended to Christian educators.

The way of looking on God and the world derived from process metaphysics is only one possibility. There is a long tradition based on various kinds of idealism that affected theological thinking in previous years and found its modern exponents in such men as William Temple and Paul Tillich, although these two men emphasized different aspects of this tradition. There is a peculiarly American tradition based on pragmatism and pluralism exemplified at its best in William James. There is a strong trend today toward existentialism, as found in the thought of Heidegger and Bultmann. There is the denial of metaphysics as part of theological thinking, as in the theology of Karl Barth. There is the attempt to come to terms with secular views of metaphysics, as in the thought of Paul van Buren and Harvey Cox. In some thinkers, these various strands are mixed.

The point to be made is that theological and metaphysical language-games are closely related. It can even be claimed that metaphysical models are basic to theological meaning and belief.[21] Theological and metaphysical assertions are attempts to speak in generalized terms about the nature of God and the

---

[20] See Daniel Day Williams, "Deity, Monarchy, and Metaphysics," Ivor Leclerc, ed., *The Relevance of Whitehead* (London: George Allen & Unwin; New York: Macmillan, 1961), p. 368.

[21] See Frederick Ferré, "Mapping the Logic of Models," op. cit., p. 85.

world, to back up the way one looks on the world in terms of some degree of coherence, consistency, and consideration of the nature of experience. For Whitehead, there is an overlapping between theology and metaphysics, although they are separate disciplines. "Rational religion," he writes, "must have recourse to metaphysics for a scrutiny of its terms. At the same time it contributes its own independent evidence which metaphysics must take account of in framing its description." [22] Both theology and metaphysics are speculative and seek to go "behind the scenes," to explain what is hidden or what is perceived by the use of concepts.[23] Such language is neither descriptive in any scientific sense nor self-involving in the religious sense. The person who uses self-involving language to speak of his faith in God, however, is led to the speculative language of theology and metaphysics in order to talk about his way of looking on God and the world.[24]

IMPLICATIONS FOR CHRISTIAN EDUCATION

Our educational task, if we accept Whitehead's view of metaphysics, is to assist the student to look on the world or the universe as a process or organism in which God is at work; to understand how God can be in our midst and yet stand behind the process as eternal and changeless. The interaction of everything can be a starting point.

With elementary grades, one might start with Tennyson's poetry:

> Flower in the crannied wall,
> I pluck you out of the crannies;—
> Hold you here, root and all, in my hand,

22 A. N. Whitehead, *Religion in the Making* (New York: Macmillan, 1926), p. 79.

23 See Victor Lowe, "The Approach to Metaphysics," Ivor Leclerc, ed., *The Relevance of Whitehead*, op. cit., p. 200.

24 See Donald D. Evans, "Differences Between Scientific and Religious Assertions," Ian G. Barbour, ed., *Science and Religion* (New York: Harper & Row, 1968), pp. 125–33.

> Little flower—but if I could understand
> What you are, root and all, and all in all,
> I should know what God and man is.[25]

As children work over the words of this poem, they may begin to see something of the interrelationships of all growing things. If they trace the flower back to the root back to the soil back to the water back to the rain back to the sky back to the sun and back to the structure of things, at some point the light may dawn and there will be a disclosure of the way in which all things work together. This order in nature points to aesthetic order, and "the aesthetic order is derived from the immanence of God." [26]

This is obviously an oversimplification, but it may start children to thinking about God as at work in the order of things and not as far off in the sky somewhere. Furthermore, it may lead to a moment of religious insight that is more than nature worship.

The yearning for a God who shares our problems is expressed in a modern version of Psalm 61:

> Don't you hear me crying, God,
> And hear what I got to say?
> Wherever we are we call ya
> When we are all bugged up about something.
>
> Help me be something better than I am
> So I can have more hope
> And be very strong
> When I should be.
>
> I'll try to live where you do
> So you can watch me.
>
> God, you know what I want and need
> And give something to live for
> To those that trust you.

---

[25] *The Poetical Works of Alfred Tennyson* (Boston: James R. Osgood & Co., 1875), p. 416.

[26] *Religion in the Making*, p. 105.

We hope you will give a long life
To people we like
And we may always remember them
'Cause they were good.
Help them to live like you want them to
And let all your good things protect them.

Then we will know we can trust you
And do what you want us to do.[27]

This is an expression of religious yearning on the part of a youngster in trouble with the law. Yet, against the background of Whitehead's concept of God, his appeal can be understood in terms of a God who participates in the life and joys and sufferings of a boy and provides a tower of strength to him. Junior high students could approach this kind of material with appreciation and depth.

A similar approach, identifying God with people in distress, is found in Robert Castle's "Litany for the Ghetto."

O God, who lives in tenements, who goes to segregated schools, who is beaten in precincts, who is unemployed . . .

Help us to know you.

O God, who is cold in the slums of winter, whose playmates are rats—four-legged ones who live with you and two-legged ones who imprison you . . .

Help us to touch you. . . .[28]

This portion reflects Matthew 25:31–46, TEV: "Whenever you refused to help one of these poor ones, you refused to help me."

---

[27] Carl F. Burke, *Treat Me Cool, Lord* (New York: Association Press, 1968), p. 71.

[28] Quoted by John A. T. Robinson, *Exploration into God* (Stanford: Stanford University Press, 1967), p. 138. Used by permission of Robert W. Castle, Jr.

John A. T. Robinson provides a biblical approach to this way of looking on God with a paraphrase of the first chapter of John:

> The clue to the universe was present from the beginning. It was to be found at the level of reality which we call God. Indeed, it was no other than God nor God than it. At that depth of reality the element of the personal was there from the start. Everything was drawn into existence through it, and there is nothing in the process that has come into being without it. Life owes its emergence to it, and life lights the path to man. It is that light which illumines the darkness of the subpersonal creation, and the darkness never succeeded in quenching it.
>
> The light was the clue to reality—the light which comes to clarity in man. Even before that it was making its way in the universe. It was already in the universe, and the whole process depended upon it, although it was not conscious of it. It came to its own in the evolution of the personal; yet persons failed to grasp it. But, to those who did, who believed in what it represented, it gave the potential of a fully personal relationship to God. For these the meaning of life was seen to rest, not simply on its biological basis, nor on the impulses of nature or the drives of history, but on the reality of God. And this divine personal principle found its embodiment in a man and took habitation in our midst. We saw its full glory, in all its utterly gracious reality—the wonderful sight of a person living in uniquely normal relationship to God, as son to father.
>
> From this fulness of life we have all received, in gifts without measure. It was law that governed the less than fully personal relationships even of man; the true, gracious reality came to expression in Jesus Christ. The ultimate reality of God no one has ever seen. But the one who has lived closest to it, in the unique relationship of son to father, he has laid it bare.[29]

This passage hardly qualifies as the poetic-simple language of Canon Drinkwater, but perhaps neither does the prologue that it paraphrases. If these two passages are placed side by side, however, by a high school or adult group, the comparison may

---

29 Ibid., p. 104.

lead to both metaphysical and religious insights. Bishop Robinson has portrayed in this paraphrase of a familiar passage the basic thrust of the Whiteheadian approach to a philosophy of religion without doing violence to the fundamental religious insight of the original. Or, at least, this might be the disclosure evoked by comparative study. In it is portrayed the call of God, the "lure" of Whitehead's concept, as well as the work of God both as immanent spirit and as a brooding purpose.

The concept of God as immanent in the process of living raises another issue, especially with those who think in terms of substance. If God is *a* person, how can he and a human person occupy the same area of space-time? On a more childish level, if God is everywhere, do I inhale him when I breathe? Spirit and breath come from the same root (*ruach*). John B. Cobb, Jr., provides an illustration which may prove illuminating to high school and college students and to adults: If we think of God and man as subjects instead of objects, the situation changes:

> My subjective experience has its own spatiotemporal standpoint. In one sense it extends out over the room and through the past as it brings a new synthesis out of the data it inherits. But it inherits these data from a particular spatiotemporal locus. Spatially, this locus seems to include much if not all of the brain. There is no reason to exclude this possibility on the grounds that the presence of my subjective experience would exclude that of the electrons or vice versa. The electrons can enjoy their subjectivity from their very limited standpoints within the brain while I am enjoying mine from the more inclusive one. Each has its self-identity independent of the other. The electronic events in my brain influence my human thought and feeling. My human thought and feeling influence some of the energy-events in my brain in ways that lead to specific bodily functioning obedient to my conscious intentions. Thus the events occupying the inclusive space and those occupying the included space act upon each other in complex ways, but they have also their distinct individuality and autonomy. They are independent as well as interdependent.

A World View and Christian Education 153

Cobb believes that this "offers us our best analogy for thinking of the spatial relation of God and the world." [30] The educational issue is that a group could struggle with this relationship until the members either fitted it into a metaphysical and theological onlook or rejected it.

The material for taking a class through the exercise of thinking metaphysically is provided in the opening sections of this chapter. For education in the religious significance of process philosophy, there are some clues in Whitehead's summary of the major elements of religious response: worship, adventure, meaning, companionship, and peace.

Worship. Religion is a vision, says Whitehead, of that "whose possession is the final good, and yet is beyond all reach." [31] "The power of God is the worship he inspires." [32] Education makes whatever is worshipful subject to thought, and the task is to analyze what it mea..s to worship God, who calls it forth. This is the central factor in religious response, and conduct is only a by-product.

Adventure. Whitehead means this in a specialized sense, in that all achievements of men and cultures tend to become dull and prosaic, and that the religious man is always pressing on to new forms of beauty not yet realized. There will be times of unrest and turmoil as a result of being captured by the vision of what might be, but God urges us on.

Meaning. Whitehead could see the meaning of life in the midst of evil and suffering. He could see all things perishing. At this level, Whitehead writes, "human life is a flash of occasional enjoyments lighting up a mass of pain and misery, a bagatelle of transient experience." [33] God, because he acts by persuasion within the finite realm and yet is the source of infinite potentials, is not responsible for the evil in the world. But he takes

---

[30] John B. Cobb, Jr., op. cit., p. 79.

[31] A. N. Whitehead, *Science and the Modern World* (New York: Macmillan, 1927), p. 275.

[32] Ibid., p. 276.

[33] Ibid., p. 275.

this evil into himself and transforms it. "Values are after all worth achieving," says Cobb, because "all things in the world are taken up into God's experience." [34] Thus, there is permanence in the midst of transience.

Companionship. Here Whitehead drops into the simple language that describes relationships. God is a "companion" who shows "tender care." This is nontechnical rather than analogical language. "He is the mirror which discloses to every creature its own greatness." [35] Such language needs to be qualified, as Ramsey suggests, but the model has its own validity. God is "the fellow-sufferer who understands." [36]

Peace. This is a dynamic concept, combining freedom from self-concern with serenity, and it comes as a gift. It comes through the vision of God, and yet is beyond man's reach. It enables one to live normally, with God in the background.

Studdert Kennedy caught the spirit of peace when he wrote:

> Peace does not mean the end of all our striving,
> Joy does not mean the drying of our tears;
> Peace is the power that comes to souls arriving
> Up to the light where God himself appears.[37]

Such a vision of the world as we are given is not guaranteed. But metaphysics is significant for religion just because it provides a basis for our understanding of the universe around us, for our acceptance of the world of sense experience, and for our capacity to look on the world as God's world. It is an onlook, and therefore performative and self-involving.

Christian education is capable of dealing with the kinds of thinking we have described in this chapter. Indeed, if it fails to do so, it also fails to provide for a way of looking on the world

---

[34] John B. Cobb, Jr., *A Christian Natural Theology* (Philadelphia: Westminster Press, 1965), p. 219. I am basing my outline of these five points on pages 216–23.

[35] Ibid., p. 220.

[36] *Process and Reality*, p. 532.

[37] G. A. Studdert Kennedy, *The Unutterable Beauty* (London: Hodder & Stoughton, 1927), p. 4. Used by permission of the publisher.

in which God is active. Because our intimations of God are so often placed within the wrong kind of world view, operating with the wrong kind of language, our students are liable to conclude that the whole story is nonsense, and therefore they are frustrated because they have no place to fit whatever visions they may have into a world view that makes sense of their visions. So their visions take them out of the church into other worlds. And in this way the church loses its case for the wrong reasons and without benefit of an accurate hearing. Maybe metaphysics is more important than we think.

X. RELIGIOUS
LANGUAGE AND
CHRISTIAN
EDUCATION

The proper use of the analytic tools of language may help us greatly in rethinking the ways and purposes of Christian education. The language of the Bible is not straightforward or descriptive when its purpose is specifically religious. If Christianity is thought of as a speech-event, giving birth to the new literary form of gospel and making use of myth, parable, story, and epistle in a distinctive way, we need to be aware of such uses in our teaching.

However, some of the early studies in language analysis warn us against too easy talk about God. The demand for verification opens up a question with which we have been concerned throughout the book. What is the empirical anchor for our beliefs? If "belief that" must precede "belief in," how do we get that way? If a disclosure is evoked, how do we distinguish it from wish-fulfillment or hallucination caused by drugs? If we can no longer think in terms of first-century mythology and world views, is there an existential or metaphysical language into which it can be translated?

We are helped here by the suggestion that there are many kinds of language-games. This can be a dangerous concept, for we may decide that astrology, spiritual mediums, insane bliks, or onlooks that are identified with God's onlook have their own validity. But the language-game concept is helpful as we try to understand ways of thinking in other cultures, not only primitive ones or those foreign to us but also the subcultures in our own country.

When we look at the language-games among the sciences, we find a methodology that is akin to metaphysical and theological thinking. The uses and meanings of words in mathematical physics, for example, begin with imageless concepts which are verified deductively in experience, although not in terms of a specific experiment. Here is a language-game which provides an accurate empirical fit to send a man to the moon or to blow up the world, and yet it is not based on sense experience and inductive logic. It is similar to metaphysics and theology in that it needs to take account of many elements in human experience by means of generalized concepts.

There is another language-game which is more dangerous because it is open to criticism on the basis of subjectivism, privacy, and wish-fulfillment. In one form, it is so private that for Whitehead religion is said to begin with what a man does with his solitariness. For Northrop, the experience of the "undifferentiated aesthetic continuum" is private, operating on the fringes of consciousness, and yet it is universally prevalent. But this is not far different from any birth of insight.

When these two language-games are brought together, as in Whitehead's way of looking on the world, we have a basis for what Ramsey calls a "cosmic disclosure." Thus we have grounds for talking about God not only in terms of what the concept of God means but in terms of God as objective reality. We have tried to clarify this kind of thinking at both the religious and metaphysical levels.

Primarily, however, we are concerned with the use of the tools of linguistic analysis to help us in Christian education. That is why the last half of each chapter points to its educational significance. It is at this point that the suggestions of

Ramsey, Bushnell, Drinkwater, and Evans are significant, with additional help from van Buren, Whitehead, Belth, and Peters. We have been seeking to understand how Christians, in terms of our twentieth-century Western, scientific, secular culture, may speak meaningfully, communicate ideas, and evoke, hopefully, disclosures of God that may lead to commitment. This specifically religious dimension of Christian education, however, needs always to be supplemented by a theological and metaphysical framework or onlook, and this leads us from the logically odd, poetic-simple forms of discourse to more complex critical analysis.

As Christian educators, our purpose is that the gospel be heard and responded to. We are concerned with what God has done, does, and hopefully will do. Much of this activity is in the form of words, words which *do* things. The tools provided by the logic of self-involvement, showing how language is performative in terms of onlooks, are essential for the church school teacher or catechist, who also needs to be alerted to the existence of both open and closed bliks. There is a gap between the secular and Christian onlooks, and although the proclamation of Jesus as the Christ and God as the Creator may be helpful, this does not provide a basis for crossing the gap unless there is a disclosure such as Ramsey proposes. Only then can we say, "We are as certain of God as we are of ourselves and other selves." [1]

This means that Christian educators will seek to enable the learner to say, "I believe," not as a ritual act or as an intellectual exercise but as the assertion of trust in another "I." [2] This is not just believing *that* God exists; it is more like asserting that I trust my wife and that I will back this assertion both with empirical evidence and active defense.[3] So when I say, "I believe

---

[1] Dallas M. High, *Language, Persons and Belief* (New York: Oxford University Press, 1967), p. 182.

[2] See ibid., p. 168.

[3] See Ian T. Ramsey, *Religious Language* (London: SCM Press, 1957; New York: Macmillan Paperback, 1963), p. 53.

in *you*, God," I am willing to stand behind my statement.

What is clear, I hope, is that study of language analysis from a philosophical point of view enables us to speak more effectively and accurately, on the basis of a carefully worked out theology and metaphysics, of God as existing, who in Christ was reconciling the world to himself, and who through the community of the Spirit is drawing all men unto him, that they by and through their faith may be recipients of his grace. Of this God, we say, "I believe *in* . . ." There will be continuing disclosure and commitment, and the resulting action will be the ministry of the church in the world.

The various language-games which are suitable to Christian education are used most effectively within situations and relationships that are provided in the classroom or the community. The key concepts of dialogue, engagement, and kerygma may prove helpful at this point.

DIALOGUE

We have already referred to the biblical use of dialogue, but we need to look again at its educational significance. Reuel L. Howe pictures dialogue as an interchange of meanings between persons, in which the proper relationship tends to break down the barriers so that meaning can flow in two directions. He builds this interpretation on the basis of Martin Buber's interpersonal relationship philosophy of "I–Thou," in which only adequate trust can be the basis for genuine dialogue between pupil and teacher. The important element is the overcoming of obstacles. The key to this understanding of dialogue is not mastering a methodology but achieving a relationship. Almost any method will work when the relationship has been established.[4]

A theory of language is related to this interpretation. Meanings of words are derived from the experience of prior relationships. One cannot even talk about dialogue until a relationship of dialogue has been established. Such basic Christian concepts

---

[4] See Reuel L. Howe, *The Miracle of Dialogue* (New York: Seabury Press, 1962), pp. 37 f.

as love, fellowship, forgiveness, justice, trust, and grace cannot be understood religiously unless there has been prior experience of these relationships on a purely human level, which can then be interpreted theologically. Therefore, to talk about God meaningfully we need experience of God at work in these relationships. When we have had these experiences in terms of a human onlook, we may be helped by the proper direction of attention to discern God at work in our midst.

This relationship of dialogue is essential to Christian education because it offers the situation in which many of the goals of Christian education may be achieved. We have just referred to an altered onlook. Because dialogue offers the opportunity for self-involvement, it makes possible a deeper probing of the person's key question of "Who am I?" Therefore, in some instances, dialogue becomes the opportunity for a changed onlook, especially when one member of the group develops a special concern and ministers to the other. This can be observed as the pattern in some specialized groups, such as Alcoholics Anonymous, in which the knowledge that someone is so concerned that he can be phoned at any time of the day or night when temptation is the greatest becomes the resource for a new way of behaving. A similar group, operating as a cell within the larger body of the congregation, provides the opportunity for the exchange of stories which increase in depth as mutual trust grows within the group, leading perhaps to what Bultmann means by "authentic existence."

Dialogue may go on in almost any circumstances. The attitudes and atmosphere are what is most important. It is a sharing of stories, of onlooks, of bliks, by which profounder onlooks may be evoked, but never for the purpose of winning a victory over another. The imperialism of the teacher is effectively destroyed by this approach, although the teacher may still be the expert, leader, or coach with the right to evaluate the process. Bushnell made a similar point when he said that all one could ever do was to stimulate another's thinking; we never put our thoughts into his head.

Dialogue, precisely because it lacks the formality of the traditional classroom, offers the opportunity to analyze the language of faith. Because of the interchange, the teacher and pupils can be more certain about the meanings of the words used, can ascertain the logically odd disclosure language of the Bible, and can try as many models and qualifiers as are necessary to make possible the evoking of a disclosure, turning to as many myths, parables, stories, and poetry as needed to aid in the process. Within the dialogue situation, the class can ignore the timetable of a syllabus and spend time enough, for example, on studying a myth to take account of its truth-value or to demythologize it and translate it into current existentialism or some other modern form of thinking. When this is achieved, as Howe suggests, with a flow of meaning in various directions, the chances of fresh onlooks occurring are very great.

ENGAGEMENT

Another key concept for Christian education is engagement. David R. Hunter has made use of it to deepen the usual meaning of "encounter" or "meeting." Two trains "encounter" one another on a bridge, with disastrous results. Two automobiles "meet" at an intersection. This language reflects a theology that conceives of God as "wholly other," as transcendent in the sense of being beyond man. Thus, Emil Brunner speaks of a "divine-human encounter." This is almost at the opposite pole from the mystics, who speak of "meeting" in terms of "union." Both views may merit similar psychological descriptions.

Engagement, in contrast to encounter, is especially helpful in avoiding both extremes of interpretation. The word carries the implication of intertwining, involvement, and response in which there is give-and-take in both directions. This engagement, like Jacob's wrestling with an angel, may seem violent, or, like Jeremiah's experience, it may be a call to obedience, or, like Pentecost, it may be the opening of good news to others.[5]

---

[5] See David R. Hunter, *Christian Education as Engagement* (New York: Seabury Press, 1963).

It seems to me that we need to look at the concept of engagement from two directions as we seek to talk about God. First, if we have been correct in our estimate of the place of relationships in the meaning of language and the framework of communication, we can carry over what we have just said about dialogue. There is, here, a way of looking on God as working through his grace in our midst; he is immanent. As we participate in experiences within a group, family, class, or congregation, and note that people seem to change their onlooks and are, in the language of the New Testament, new creations or born anew or transformed or made new in Christ, we look on this as the work of God in our midst. Here then is interpersonal engagement which is human and more.

The second direction from which to look at engagement is from our belief in God who is directly known. If we believe that our metaphysical concepts include God as a reality, on grounds similar to those proposed by Northrop, Whitehead, and Hartshorne, then we can take seriously talk about engagement with God through the experience of the "undifferentiated aesthetic continuum," which means that on the fringes of our consciousness there is the experience of what William James called the "divine more," [6] and this disclosure is correlated with our concept of God as postulated in our abstract thinking.

Our study of religious language allows for both uses of the word engagement. Ramsey's emphasis on disclosure language, the logically odd assertions that lead to the evoking of discernment or insight, which he calls a cosmic disclosure, comes close to what we have just said about engagement with God. The "language of the heart" about which Drinkwater speaks is the same type of usage. If, with Evans, we are to look on God's glory, this again is the onlook that makes such language possible. If it is the experience of men in their solitude, as Whitehead suggests, it still has to be worked out in language in the community of believers.

---

[6] See William James, *The Varieties of Religious Experience* (New York: Longmans, Green & Co., 1902), p. 508.

Both dialogue and engagement point linguistically to the proclamation of the gospel, which is the source of Christian belief in God and in the meaning of life. Unless the kerygma stands at the center of the Christian revelation, we are not being true to a tradition that stands on the Bible, tradition, and human experience.

KERYGMA

Christian teaching finds its source in the kerygma, that proclamation or story of what God has done in history and uniquely in Jesus Christ, leading to the establishing of a community centering in Christ. Attempts have been made to distinguish between kerygma as telling the story and didache as moral teaching based on the story, with C. H. Dodd as a key scholar,[7] but for Christian education the distinction is difficult to maintain (if indeed it is valid).

For a brief time, the phrase "kerygmatic catechetics" was popular among Roman Catholic educators.[8] It served its purpose in its emphasis on kerygma as a means for getting away from didactic teaching, making room for the proper mapping of religious language in teaching. If poetic-simple is a clue to religious teaching, then the catechism properly belongs in the hands of the teacher, as a summary in scientific-simple of what is proclaimed. The Bible is understood as a story of God's mighty acts, a record of the ways in which God has revealed himself and men have appropriated the revelation. It is important, therefore, that this story be told not only in parts but in its completeness, and in such a way that it opens up to the student the possibility of response in terms of decision, commitment, and faith.

This emphasis on a biblical onlook centering in the kerygma

---

[7] See C. H. Dodd, *The Apostolic Preaching* (New York: Harper & Bros., 1936), pp. 3–6.

[8] See Gerard S. Sloyan, ed., *Modern Catechetics* (New York: Macmillan, 1963).

fits in with most of the approaches we have considered. The central factor in this approach is the story, told in such a way, with the proper mapping of language, that there may be a response, even a change in onlook. David Hunter places the emphasis on the story as a way of opening up the religious issues in the lives of the students and their problems in decision-making, and these are correlated with stories that will help them grasp the meaning of these issues in terms of the Christian faith. The story comes first, and then the interpretations, and finally the propositions. The possibility of a disclosure lies in the story and not in the propositions.

From the point of view of some of the linguistic philosophers, this conclusion seems too pat. It is too much like a slightly stepped-up Bible class. It places the responsibility for the story on the teacher and the source in the Bible. If Ramsey is right, the logically odd phrases which make a disclosure possible may come from all kinds of theological discourse. The words to point to God, such as "infinitely good" or "all powerful" or "creator *ex nihilo*," are found in propositions and not in Bible stories. The stories may help to make the "ice break," but so may a consideration of the logically odd qualifiers, or even, as Braithwaite suggests, stories from almost any source.

If we consider dialogue, engagement, and kerygma in this manner, we are led to conclude that the curriculum is broader than any formal course of study. If we move in an existential direction, we may agree with David Hunter that religious issues provide the organizing principle; or, if we follow Schubert Ogden, we may seek an existential understanding of "authentic existence" and also look on God and his world as objective and worth metaphysical consideration; or, if we follow Marc Belth, we may be "concerned with the development of the powers of thinking, symbol manipulation, and the identification of theoretical bases for acting and speaking . . ."; in any case, we have a story to tell. The concern of the educator is that a biblical onlook should be a live option, no matter how it is demythologized or adapted so that assertions about the biblical faith have currency in today's world. This will lead to self-involving, performative language that does not misfire.

Insofar as discernment is evoked and commitment results, the student comes to an understanding of the church's mission. He becomes an apostle, one who is sent forth, wherever he is, to speak out and to act out his insight and his commitment. His own sphere of influence is his mission. H. Richard Niebuhr wrote that the major task of the church is "the increase of the love of God and neighbor," [9] and from some points of view these commands may be identical rather than equal. We do not select our neighbor, for he is whoever we happen to meet. We are to be in dialogue with our neighbor, to enter into engagement with him, and to share in such a way that the kerygma may be noted and responded to.

This leads us to take seriously the idea that Jesus Christ came to save the world. "In Christ God was reconciling the world to himself (2 Cor. 5:19)." There is no distinction between the sacred and the secular, for the doctrine of creation stresses that it is world-creation that we are talking about. This is the locale of the church at work. Robert Clyde Johnson writes that "the unavoidable, primal fact is that the church is in the world and the world is in the church." [10] This is where we believe God located his church and where we must be if we are to fulfill our discipleship. The religious issues in our lives come alive in the work and play of our life in the world.

This summary of the significance of dialogue, engagement, and kerygma as they relate to curriculum, mission, and world leads to the following as a possible statement about Christian education: It means, then, *telling the story of God's mighty*

---

[9] H. Richard Niebuhr, *The Purpose of the Church and Its Ministry* (New York: Harper and Row, 1956), p. 31. See 1 John 4:20–21, NEB: "But if a man says, 'I love God,' while hating his brother, he is a liar. If he does not love his brother whom he has seen, it cannot be that he loves God whom he has not seen. And indeed this command comes to us from Christ himself: that he who loves God must also love his brother."

[10] Robert Clyde Johnson, ed., *The Church and Its Changing Ministry* (Philadelphia: United Presbyterian Church, 1961), p. 9.

acts in such a way that the listener participates in the dialogue by telling his own story, and he comes into an engagement with God and his fellows in his daily life, and therefore the meaning of his life is disclosed to him in a new way, and through commitment to God in Christ he is reborn daily as he lives as a Christian in community in the world.

The key words in the above statement are performatives, and the new onlook is a gift of disclosure or insight, made possible because a blik or onlook has been renewed or transformed. With the discernment that leads to a new or renewed commitment must go understanding. A transformed or renewed onlook must be undergirded by empirical fit and rational concepts, resulting in theological and metaphysical thinking, either at an elementary or more advanced level.

For this result to occur in a Christian context, the empirical anchor, as Ramsey suggests, may be found in worship, and worship, like other forms of religious language, has its own language-game. To that problem we turn.

WORSHIP

Little has been done by anyone on the language of worship, beyond the claim that it is the empirical anchor for some religious assertions. Liturgical language is encrusted with tradition and often fails to speak even to the remnant of the faithful, much less to anyone else (except possibly to God himself). Not only is there obsolescence, but there is failure to provide those occasions for disclosure, discernment, and insight which are essential for renewed commitment and obedience.

One of the problems is that many liturgical phrases, although quite properly biblical in intent, are based on the King James or earlier versions of the Bible, and therefore they have an archaic or quaint or awkward quality that makes any meaningful participation difficult. Many key phrases of traditional prayers are either misleading or unintelligible. Take the familiar phrase from the Lord's Prayer, "Lead us not into temptation." It has been translated, "Do not bring us to the test

(NEB)," "Keep us clear of temptation (P)," "Do not bring us to hard testing (TEV)." If this phrase is taken literally against the background of the coming of the kingdom, how can we demythologize it so that it makes any sense in today's world with its sense of continuity? If we believe that the time of testing will be the end of the world, when God brings in his kingdom, we can say the words without difficulty. No literal translation can bring out the meaning for the modern man. Should we then make our own paraphrase in terms of a different view of history? Should we say: "Keep us from losing our faith in you"? [11]

We have the same kind of problem with "Do this in remembrance of me." Is the Holy Communion service simply a meeting of the "Jesus Memorial Society"? Or can we state more effectively what was meant: "When you do this, I will be present"? Is there here, as Schubert Ogden would say, an act of re-presentation? If so, our liturgical phrases do not say so.

Does blood still suggest cleansing properties? Are we "washed in the blood of the lamb?" Or what does it mean when the priest quotes Jesus: "This is my blood"? What potency do we believe that blood has today, except as plasma? Does eating the body suggest a form of spiritual cannibalism?

Traditionalists may respond to such criticisms with the comment that only the initiated can understand the biblical symbolism of worship, and the problem of education is to help people learn this liturgical language. This has been the position of most liturgical scholars and of the churches. Children are exposed to traditional worship and nurtured in it until it becomes second nature to them, or they rebel against the whole system.

Attempts have been made to update the various liturgies, not always with much success. When the Roman Church began to translate the Mass from Latin to English, what surprised many people was the flatness of the translation. What might be called the "liturgical tone" was lacking, somewhat as an opera

---

[11] See John C. Kirby, *Word and Action* (New York: Seabury Press, 1969), pp. xiv–xviii.

translated from Italian or German into English loses its "style." A comparison of recent English mass texts with the *Book of Common Prayer* suggests one of the major difficulties. When Cranmer translated from the Latin in the sixteenth century, he had available in the common language of the people a kind of rhythmic prose that could be read aloud to evoke a worshipful response. When this prose is analyzed, as it has been by John Suter, it is seen to be a form similar to what Canon Drinkwater calls poetic-simple. This rhythmic prose, carefully balanced in its cadences, with a specific format especially in those prayers called "collects," is meant to be read aloud. Many of Cranmer's prayers are now archaic, but they can serve as a model of the way in which modern prayers might be written. What is needed is the genius of a Cranmer! [12]

The psalms, as early hymns, also are in poetic-simple. The current generation has been more successful in writing modern psalms than modern prayers. Many of the recent folk songs combine verse and guitar as the early psalms combined Hebrew parallelism and the harp. We are not far off the beam with some of the new hymns, both those that are somewhat traditional and some that are closer to the rhythms of the secular world.[13]

Most of the experiments in rewriting the liturgy seek some clarification and more dramatic movement, but they are primarily traditional. One experiment that breaks new ground is by William Birmingham, "An Urban Liturgy of Identity." At the beginning, it reminds us of some of the attempts of linguistic analysts to speak of God:

> *Priest* What is the name of God?
> *All* I am Who I am.
> *Priest* What is the name of God?
> *All* I am Yahweh and there is no other.

---

[12] See John W. Suter, *The Book of English Collects* (New York: Harper & Bros., 1940), pp. xxvii–xxxvi.

[13] See *RISK: New Hymns for a New Day* (Geneva: Youth Departments of the World Council of Churches and World Council of Christian Education), II, No. 3, 1966.

Priest What is the name of God?
All   I exist.
Priest What is the name of God?
All   I am He Who blots out transgressions.
Priest His people shall know His name.
        They shall know that He
        is He who speaks.[14]

The remainder of the service is mostly readings from modern translations of the Gospel of John, with a dramatic sharing of the Holy Communion as the climax. It is a step in the right direction.

The language of address to God has been moving from "thou" to "you." This is to avoid quaintness, and in English the "you" can be singular or plural. In other languages, the equivalent of "thou" is personal and singular, and the equivalent of "you" is more formal. But we are limited to English, and it should be "the language of the heart." We do not use "thou" when speaking to an intimate friend, a spouse, or child. Why should we do so with God? Or maybe we should be more formal with God, and the easy-going "you" fails to catch the element of the holy. But "thou" leads to verbal forms such as "hast" or "wouldst" or "makest" or other awkward and artificial English words. We need more experiments before we decide which kinds of prayer are most useful.[15]

Such experiments are sure to multiply the ways in which people worship. This may be a good thing, provided it does not increase the scandals of our divisions. For we need to learn how

---

[14] Quoted in *Word and Action* (New York: Seabury Press; © 1969 The Anglican Church of Canada), p. 191. Copyright, William Birmingham. Used by permission.

[15] Examples of modern prayers can be found in such books as Malcolm Boyd, *Are You Running with Me, Jesus?* (New York: Holt, Rinehart & Winston, 1965), Michel Quoist, *Prayers of Life* (London: Gill & Son, 1963), Omer Tanghe, *Prayers from Life* (New York: P. J. Kenedy & Sons, 1968). For an overview on worship and education see Paul H. Vieth, *Worship in Christian Education* (Philadelphia: United Church Press, 1965).

to use religious language to bring the churches together so that their ministry in the world will be more effective.

ECUMENICAL EDUCATION

One serious reason why the churches have failed to communicate more effectively has been their divided status. Albert van den Heuvel has said that "the ecumenical movement is a laboratory where sick churches try to discover how to get well together." [16] Even the word ecumenical has many meanings. Some Protestants were misled when the Vatican II Council was called "ecumenical" because they saw the meaning of the word from the perspective of the World Council of Churches. Some people see its meaning in terms of mergers, others in a return to Rome, others in a loose federation, others in terms of social and political action in the world. Much of what is called "ecumenical," such as the study of the positions of other churches or the bringing of people together for mutual understanding, is properly "pre-ecumenical." Sharing in the mission of God in the world is a true ecumenical activity, a kind of "secular ecumenicity" where "only those fully committed to the abolition of hunger may receive communion, only those who are fully committed to unity in the world may work for unity between the churches, only those who are fully committed to real communication between estranged people may pray, and only those willing to die for their fellows may carry the message of the resurrection." [17] These are strong words, but they communicate a challenge. The ecumaniac is using "ecumenicity" as a performative, and his blik is showing in his careless disregard of the consequences.

The starting point is the development of an attitude, an ecumenical mentality, an onlook in which a person has, says Cardinal Bea, "a constant vision of the whole of Christianity in the whole world and in all confessions, and shapes his work ac-

---

[16] "Secular Ecumenicity and the Teaching of the Faith," *Religious Education*, LXII (Mar.–Apr. 1967), p. 121.

[17] Ibid., pp. 126, 224.

cording to this vision. He respects everyone, listens to all, and considers their problems as his own. From such a consideration of all those who are baptized in Christ or at least believe in him, we become more and more conscious of the problems presented by the wounded condition of a divided Christianity." [18]

The local congregation or parish is usually incapable of achieving an ecumenical mentality, much less an approach to ecumenical action. It is irresponsible to get an individual Christian excited about the ecumenical mission to the world and to leave him alone to be crucified. Yet if the individual is not concerned about his neighbors, he does not know that the world for him is his neighborhood. If he does not see the connection between his daily life, which is secular, and his faith, his Christian education is a failure. This support for him must be on a wider basis than the local congregation, for when groups of Christians share their activities they can be more effective. It is no accident that witness against racial discrimination is always more effective when a council of churches is involved or there is an interfaith witness.[19]

The vocabulary of the ecumenical movement, although often buried in the strange jargon of committee language, is at times a vehicle for communication. More often, everyday language, used by laymen as they face the problems of the world, provides dynamic insight and the possibility of commitment, as we see in the development of lay academies and other specialized lay training centers, where men and women from many occupations and denominations seek together to find out what their responsibilities are as Christians in their work.[20]

---

[18] In Samuel H. Miller and G. Ernest Wright, eds., *Ecumenical Dialogue at Harvard: The Roman Catholic-Protestant Colloquium* (Cambridge: The Belknap Press of Harvard University, 1964), p. 31.

[19] See Randolph C. Miller, "The Challenge of the Ecumenical Movement to Church Education," Kendig Brubaker Cully, ed., *The Episcopal Church and Education* (New York: Morehouse-Barlow Co., 1966), pp. 227–40.

[20] See Lee J. Gable, *Church and World Encounter* (Philadelphia: United Church Press, 1964).

If people are to work together as Christians, the educational process must include study, discussion, worship, and work. The focus needs to be on imagination, for what we need most are new ways to meet new occasions in today's world. We do not yet know what it is we need to do to fulfill God's plan for the world. We know that war must cease, populations must be limited in their growth, poverty must be overcome, educational opportunities must be provided on a wider basis, and that people must be free to hear the good news of salvation through Jesus Christ, but these are such tremendous and complex problems that we do not know where to start. It has been suggested that unless a new Augustine or Luther emerges to bring about a new reformation, nothing much will happen. But we cannot wait for someone else. The responsibility is ours, and if we lack the stature of an Augustine or a Luther, we have the stature that God gave us.[21]

Why All These Words?

We come now to the end of our study of religious language. We have used a great variety of words, some of them in common use and some of them specialized and even invented for a particular purpose. Some of these words overlap in their meanings and may even be almost synonymous. Word substitution helps one to avoid being caught in a one-word situation, where the defense of the word becomes more important than the meaning to which it may point. Substitution of one word for another is never adequate, but such action may be valid and intelligible in order to communicate, as in the case of faith-decision-trust-commitment-loyalty, etc. There are shades of difference in this series, but if I use faith-know-belief that, I have obviously started with a different use of faith, or I have moved in a direction that distorts the original meaning in favor of my

---

[21] See the two symposia on "The Ecumenical Revolution and Religious Education," *Religious Education*, LXI (Sept.–Oct. 1966) and LXII (Mar.–Apr. 1967).

own theological blik.[22] This forces us from dependence on definition to a study of use as a basis for meaning. We want to be sure how a word is used in a sentence, preferably in an example (paradigm case) that is clear, and then we can understand its meaning in a more difficult situation. The test of a synonym is whether it can operate in the same or a similar sentence without distortion.[23]

We have, for example, used the words blik, onlook, disclosure, discernment, insight, revelation in similar ways. I can say, "I have a blik about my wife's cooking," or "I look on my wife's cooking as good for my health," or "My wife's cooking is a disclosure of her love," or "My wife's cooking led me to the discernment of tastes I never suspected were possible," or "I had no insight into the delights of French cooking until my wife bought a French cookbook," or "My wife's latest cooking adventure was a revelation." These words, obviously are not synonyms, and they have not been used with the same grammatical structure, but they belong to a family of words necessary to cover my intellectual and intuitive grasp of the total concept, "my wife's cooking," and the subject is still far from exhausted.

I can attempt to share this knowledge with another by using language similar to the above, by inviting him to dinner, or by suggesting that he buy his wife a French cookbook, at which point I may run into his blik, onlook, discernment, or insight concerning his wife's cooking. If I am reduced to a one-word approach to describe my wife's cooking, I cannot convey the complexity of this relatively simple operation.

Let us assume that I invite my friend to dinner. The conversation about my wife's cooking has only pointed at something, and now he has certain expectations because he has had previous experience with various foods. My language so far has been self-involving and performative about my wife, and my invitation to him is also self-involving and performative. Now he

---

[22] See James Barr, *The Semantics of Biblical Language* (London: Oxford University Press, 1961), pp. 215–16, 256.

[23] See ibid., p. 266.

accepts. But I have invited him for three days hence. How do we know that the invitation will still be valid, or that he will respond by showing up? Our language at this point assumes the kind of thinking that provides for continuity and dependable prediction, which is based on the use of imageless postulation.[24]

My friend comes to dinner. Afterward he says, "I agree with you. I look on your wife as an excellent cook," and he adds, "and a gracious hostess. You didn't tell me that." Here is an additional, unexpected disclosure, and he expresses himself in the performative language of self-involvement: "I would like my wife to be able to cook like yours, and to be as gracious." A behavioral-postural attitude is now developing.

This kind of language is perfectly ordinary and normal. Yet it is making use of many of the aspects of language which we use when we speak of God. This dinner illustration, built out of disclosure language and its close relatives among bliks and onlooks, with the self-involving performative element, may lead us to see that we have similar obligations when we invite people to church or to participate in a Christian education program.

What might be called the religious diet of the church will be analogous to my wife's cooking, and the way it is presented will be in as gracious a manner as she is a hostess. Only in this way will such phrases as "Drink of me" come alive. If the model of Jesus as the water of life is to have currency, this is the kind of approach we must have in mind. If we use the model of "the

---

[24] Says Northrop: "No words can mean or say anything, except as one knows, with inexpressible and unsayable immediacy, what the words are pointing at or showing, independently of the words themselves. Such knowledge is what the word mystical means. . . . The other and quite different species of mysticism is that of imageless intellectual immediacy or intuition, which concept by intellection sentences and their formal syntax self-show, but can neither point at nor say." The former leaves untouched one's "belief in the constancy of his determinate personality through time or in eternal objects in a public spatiotemporal world. It also leaves meaningless the legal person who is obligated today by a contract he entered into yesterday." This depends on the latter approach. *Man, Nature and God* (New York: Pocket Books, Inc., 1962), pp. 241–43.

body and blood of Christ" in the Holy Communion, this disclosure language is essential. But more than words is necessary,
for words only point at or show the reality which is the source
of our spiritual nourishment. We must be able to say, "Taste
and eat."

Talk surrounds both the dinner and the sacraments. Such
speaking may add a depth dimension to what is being experienced. Or the talk may seem trivial. Or it may be a conversation in a foreign tongue. However, the language may make
possible the appropriating of the meaning of the meal or the
sense of community, if it is sufficiently suitable in terms of providing insight through its models and logically odd qualifiers.
At some point, it is hoped that the light will dawn and the
diner will recognize who is his host.

Just as the guest at the dinner participates in these ways, the
guest or student or worshiper in church responds with new discernment and commitment, so that we may speak of intuition,
religious experience, God's grace, or the "undifferentiated aesthetic continuum" as the nourishing element, and the self-involving language of deep caring, commitment, faith, trust, and
obedience as response. One's way of looking on God and the
world is either strengthened or changed. So we begin to agree
that if the invitation is genuine, if the steak is as promised, if
the word is such that the invitation is accepted in fact, and if as
a result there are new disclosure and commitment, there is an
empirical anchor in such feeding of the flock, an empirical fit
that provides verification sufficient to make one return for as
many meals as possible, for here is where one finds "the way, the
truth, and the life."

After one has been fed, especially when it is the bread of
life, he is enabled to fulfill his responsibilities. The church which
has gathered for the feast scatters so that its members may live
out their vocations, meet their commitments to others, obey
their ethical and social obligations wherever they happen to be,
and show forth a Christian style of life.

No illustration can be forced to carry the full weight of the argument of this book, just as no parable can reflect the full power of the gospel, and no one word (not even love) can summarize the meaning of God. But we can say with the observers of the early church, "Behold how they love one another." I can say with Paul, "So I fight, and not as a shadow boxer." Just as new occasions teach new duties, so new disclosures mean new commitments, and new onlooks involve one in new performatives.

BOOKS TO READ

I. Introductory Critical Surveys

Ferré, Frederick. *Language, Logic, and God.* New York: Harper & Row, 1962.

Martin, James A., Jr. *The New Dialogue Between Philosophy and Theology.* New York: Seabury Press, 1966. These two books provide the background information on the whole field of religious language.

II. Books on Religious Language of Primary Interest for This Study

Evans, Donald. *The Logic of Self-Involvement.* London: SCM Press, 1963; New York: Herder & Herder, 1969. An original and perceptive study of performative language, following J. L. Austin, applied to the biblical concept of creation.

Flew, Antony, and MacIntyre, Alasdair, eds. *New Essays in Philosophical Theology.* London: SCM Press, 1955. Brilliant early essays that discuss language about God, mostly from a negative perspective.

High, Dallas M. *Language, Persons, and Belief.* New York: Oxford University Press, 1967. A careful study of Wittgenstein's later writings, with constructive suggestions from William H. Poteat, worked out in a new synthesis.

————, ed. *New Essays on Religious Language.* New York: Oxford University Press, 1969. A collection of hard to find essays by Paul Holmer, Ian T. Ramsey, Frederick Ferré, William H. Poteat, and others.

179

Northrop, F. S. C. *Man, Nature and God.* New York: Pocket Books, Inc., 1962. A careful and technical analysis of scientific and religious knowledge based on the use of language and logic.

Ogden, Schubert M. *Christ Without Myth.* New York: Harper & Bros., 1961.

———. *The Reality of God and Other Essays.* New York: Harper & Row, 1966. Ogden deals with Bultmann's position and builds his own position in a broader theological and philosophical perspective.

Ramsey, Ian T. *Religious Language.* London: SCM Press, 1957; New York: Macmillan Paperback, 1963.

———. *Models and Mystery.* London: Oxford University Press, 1964.

———. *Christian Discourse.* London: Oxford University Press, 1965. Ramsey provided the first serious and original thinking of a constructive nature derived from logical empiricism.

Religious Education. 545 W. 111th St., New York, N.Y. 10025. See "Linguistic Philosophy and Religious Education," a symposium by Paul M. van Buren, Ian T. Ramsey, Gordon Kaufman, Frederick Ferré, Paul Holmer, and others, Jan.–Feb. 1965; R. C. Miller, "Linguistic Models and Religious Education," July–Aug. 1966, pp. 269–78; David B. McIlhiney, "Paul van Buren and the Christian Stories," Jan.–Feb. 1967, pp. 32–37.

Smith, H. Shelton, ed. *Horace Bushnell.* London and New York: Oxford University Press, 1965. Contains Bushnell's "Dissertation on Religious Language."

Van Buren, Paul M. *The Secular Meaning of the Gospel.* New York: Macmillan, 1963. A thorough use of the verification principle applied to language about God.

———. *Theological Explorations.* London: SCM Press; New York: Macmillan, 1968. Occasional essays, including one on Christian education.

Wittgenstein, Ludwig. *Philosophical Investigations.* 2d ed.; New York: Macmillan, 1958. A fundamental book in the field, reflecting the author's later thinking.

III. Other Studies and Approaches to Religious Language

Barr, James. *Semantics of Biblical Language*. London: Oxford University Press, 1961. Warns of many misuses of biblical language.

Bultmann, Rudolf. *Jesus Christ and Mythology*. New York: Charles Scribner's Sons, 1958. One among many helpful writings by Bultmann.

Cobb, John B., Jr. *A Christian Natural Theology*. Philadelphia: Westminster Press, 1965. An application of Whitehead's philosophy.

Hartshorne, Charles. *The Divine Relativity: A Social Conception of God*. New Haven, Conn.: Yale University Press, 1948. All of Hartshorne's writings are significant for thinking about God and a world view.

Hick, John. *Faith and Knowledge*. 2d ed.; Ithaca, N.Y.: Cornell University Press, 1957, 1966. A careful analysis of the meaning of faith; verification after death a possibility.

Lewis, H. D., ed. *Clarity Is Not Enough*. London: George Allen & Unwin, 1963; New York: Humanities Press, 1963. Philosophical criticisms of some aspects of linguistic philosophy. See essay by Brand Blanshard.

Mascall, E. L. *The Secularisation of Christianity*. London: Darton, Longman & Todd, 1965. Criticisms of van Buren, Ogden, Robinson, John Knox, and others.

Meland, Bernard E., ed. *The Future of Empirical Theology*. Chicago: University of Chicago Press, 1969. Covers the Chicago school of empirical theology, and looks to the future through articles by Ogden, Cobb, Loomer, Meland, and others.

Minor, William S., ed. *Charles Hartshorne and Henry Nelson Wieman*. Carbondale, Ill.: Foundation for Creative Philosophy, 1969. Critical evaluations of Hartshorne and Wieman and their responses.

Ramsey, Ian T. *Freedom and Immortality*. London: SCM Press, 1960.

―――. *On Being Sure in Religion*. London: The Athlone Press, 1963.

―――. *Religion and Science*. London: SPCK, 1964.

————, ed. *Biology and Personality*. Oxford: Basil Blackwood, 1965.

————, ed. *Christian Ethics and Contemporary Philosophy*. London: SCM Press, 1966.

————, ed. *Prospect for Metaphysics*. London: George Allen & Unwin, 1961; New York: Philosophical Library, 1961. Further enrichment of Ramsey's thought, plus symposia by various scholars with similar viewpoints.

Richard, Robert L. *Secularization Theology*. New York: Herder & Herder, 1967. Brilliant coverage of the topic by a Roman Catholic scholar, who died before publication.

Ryle, Gilbert. *The Concept of Mind*. London: Hutchinson & Co., 1949; Peregrine Books, 1963. Exposures of "category mistakes" and a positive reconstruction of a theory of knowledge.

Sloyan, Gerard S., ed. *Shaping the Christian Message*. New York: Macmillan, 1958. The revolution in Roman Catholic catechetics. Includes Drinkwater's essay on the use of words.

Whitehead, Alfred North. *Religion in the Making*. New York: Macmillan, 1926. A classic study of the basis for religious beliefs.

Wilder, Amos N. *The Language of the Gospels: Early Christian Rhetoric*. New York: Harper & Row, 1964. The literary forms and rhetoric of the Gospels.

Wisdom, John. *Paradox and Discovery*. Oxford: Basil Blackwell, 1965. Many real facts and problems cannot be given a final linguistic form.

IV. Key Books in Education Related to the Issues of Communication and Language

Archambault, Reginald D., ed. *Philosophical Analysis and Education*. London: Routledge & Kegan Paul, 1965. Essays based on linguistic studies by English experts.

Belth, Marc. *Education as a Discipline*. Boston: Allyn & Bacon, 1965. A model of education as a distinctive subject for study.

Chamberlin, J. Gordon. *Freedom and Faith*. Philadelphia: Westminster Press, 1965. Study of three Christian educators, with concluding essay on a new model.

Cully, Iris V. *Imparting the Word*. Philadelphia: Westminster

Press, 1963. The use of biblical scholarship in Christian teaching.

Cully, Kendig Brubaker, ed. *The Westminster Dictionary of Christian Education.* Philadelphia: Westminster Press, 1963. A magnificent source book on current thinking.

De Wire, Harry. *The Christian as Communicator.* Philadelphia: Westminster Press, 1960. Some problems in communication.

Goldman, Ronald. *Religious Thinking from Childhood to Adolescence.* London: Routledge & Kegan Paul, 1963; New York: Seabury Press, 1968.

————. *Readiness for Religion.* London: Routledge & Kegan Paul, 1965; New York: Seabury Press, 1968. These studies are based on research into the use of language by children, using Piaget's categories.

Howe, Reuel L. *Man's Need and God's Action.* New York: Seabury Press, 1953.

————. *The Miracle of Dialogue.* New York: Seabury Press, 1962. Words and relationships are inseparable in communication.

Hunter, David R. *Christian Education as Engagement.* New York: Seabury Press, 1963. Centers on religious issues in life as the organizing principle for Christian education.

Jahsmann, Allan Hart. *Power Beyond Words.* St. Louis: Concordia Publishing House, 1969. A summary in simple terms of some of the best thinking in Christian education.

Little, Sara. *The Role of the Bible in Contemporary Christian Education.* Richmond: John Knox Press, 1961. One of the best comparative studies of major approaches to teaching the Bible.

Madge, Violet. *Children in Search of Meaning.* London: SCM Press, 1965. How children actually talk about God.

Miller, Randolph C. *The Clue to Christian Education.* New York: Charles Scribner's Sons, 1950.

————. *Biblical Theology and Christian Education.* New York: Charles Scribner's Sons, 1956.

————. *Christian Nurture and the Church.* New York: Charles Scribner's Sons, 1961.

————. *Education for Christian Living.* Rev. ed.; Englewood Cliffs, N.J.: Prentice-Hall, 1963.

Moran, Gabriel. *Catechesis of Revelation.* New York: Herder & Herder, 1966.

————. *Vision and Tactics.* New York: Herder & Herder, 1968. Relating theory and practice.

Nelson, C. Ellis. *Where Faith Begins.* Richmond: John Knox Press, 1967. How to develop trust in the God revealed in the Bible.

Peters, R. S. *Ethics and Education.* London: George Allen & Unwin, 1966. Value norms are introduced into the theory of education as initiation.

Sloyan, Gerard S. *Speaking of Religious Education.* New York: Herder & Herder, 1968. Occasional essays in teaching religion at various levels.

————, ed. *Modern Catechetics.* New York: Macmillan, 1963. The revolution in Roman Catholic educational theory.

Smith, J. W. D. *Religious Education in a Secular Setting.* London: SCM Press, 1969. Problems of religious language, moral education, and religious dimensions of living acutely examined.

Vieth, Paul H. *Worship in Christian Education.* Philadelphia: United Church Press, 1965. The centrality of worship in genuine Christian nurture.

Wilson, John; Williams, Norman; and Sugarman, Barry. *Introduction to Moral Education.* London: Penguin Books, 1967. Reports on research sponsored by the Farmington Trust at Oxford. Sophisticated and important study.

Wyckoff, D. Campbell. *Theory and Design in Curriculum Construction.* Philadelphia: Westminster Press, 1961. Guidelines for creating effective lesson materials.

Index

(**Bold-faced** numerals indicate the more important items.)

81, **87**, 89, 91, 100, 120, 129, 155, 158, 161   aim of, 101, 110   purpose of, **87–88**, 104, 115, 130–31, **166–67**

Goldman, Ronald, 33, 37, 57–58, 76
Gospel, **7–8**
Gospel of John (Fourth), 7, 11, 13, 84, 170

Hamilton, Peter, 49, 146
Hare, R. M., 29, 126–30
Hartshorne, Charles, xiv, 9, 40, **47–50**, 54, 68, 105, 146, 163
Heidegger, Martin, 65, 67, 148
Hepburn, Ronald, 104–5
Hick, John, 52n, 53n, 131n
High, Dallas M., 27n, 31n, 86n, 118, 119n, 143n, 145n, 159n
High school student, 73, 75, **133–34**, 153
Hinduism, 43
Historie, 66, 71, 74
Holy Communion, 122, 168, 170, 176
Holy Spirit, 95, 125, 160
Honest to God, 112
Hordern, William, 26n
Hosea, 138
How to Do Things with Words, 125
Howe, Reuel L., xv, 11, 87, 91, 112, **160, 162**
Hudson, W. D., 86n
Humor, 139
Hunter, David R., xv, 71, 162, 165

"I," 80, 86, 144–45, 159
Identity crisis, 123
Ignatius of Antioch, 5
Imageless thinking, 42–43, 158, 175
Immanent, immanence, 63, 70
Indoctrination, 36
Initiation, education as, **139–40**
Insight, 54, 82, 91 (see *Disclosure*)
Integrative concepts, 144
Intuition(s), 48, 50, 95   conspicuous, 48, 54–55
"I"-talk, 80, 86, 118, 145

Moran, Gabriel, 140
Moses, 70
Muslims, 75
Mystery, 34, 82, 106, 142, 145
Mystic(s), 23, 50, 99, 162
Mystical, 45, 175n
Mysticism, 43, 45
Myth, **16–17**, 33, **62–76**, 90, 106   meaning of, 16, 63, 69–70
    truth value of, 62, 71

Narrative mode, 107
Nathan, 138
Nature, 44
Navahos, 3
Neidhart, Walter, 123
Neighbor, 166
Nelson, C. Ellis, 126n
New Testament, 6, 10, 15, 63–64
Nicholson, Margaret, 14n
Niebuhr, H. Richard, 63n, 166
Niebuhr, Reinhold, 62, 71
Nirvana, 43
Northrop, F. S. C., xiv, 3n, 40, **41–45**, 47–50, 54–55, 58–59, 105,
    128, 158, 163, 175n
Nurture, 100, 132

Ogden, Schubert M., xv, 31n, 49, 60, 63n, 64n, 65n, 66n, **67–70,**
    72–76, 146, 165, 168
Old Testament, 6, 10, 107
Oman, John, 87
Onlook(s), **115–19**, 124–25, **130–33**, 136–38, 140, 143, 155, 159,
    161, 163, 167, 174   analogical, 116   biblical, 123–24, 131,
    164–65   Christian, 124, 133, 159   literal, 116   non-lit-
    eral, 116   parabolic, 116–17, 120, 130   religious, 116, 130
Oral transmission, 6, 8
Orwell, George, 24